**New Directions for
Child and Adolescent
Development**

Lene Arnett Jensen
Reed W. Larson
EDITORS-IN-CHIEF

William Damon
FOUNDING EDITOR

Child Development in Africa: Views From Inside

Robert Serpell
Kofi Marfo
EDITORS

Number 146 • Winter 2014
Jossey-Bass
San Francisco

CHILD DEVELOPMENT IN AFRICA: VIEWS FROM INSIDE
Robert Serpell, Kofi Marfo (eds.)
New Directions for Child and Adolescent Development, no. 146
Lene Arnett Jensen, Reed W. Larson, Editors-in-Chief

© 2014 Wiley Periodicals, Inc., A Wiley Company. All rights reserved.

No part of this publication may be reproduced, stored in a retrieval system, or transmitted in any form or by any means, electronic, mechanical, photocopying, recording, scanning, or otherwise, except as permitted under Sections 107 or 108 of the 1976 United States Copyright Act, without either the prior written permission of the Publisher or authorization through payment of the appropriate per-copy fee to the Copyright Clearance Center, 222 Rosewood Drive, Danvers, MA 01923; (978) 750-8400, fax (978) 646-8600. Requests to the Publisher for permission should be addressed to the Permissions Department, John Wiley & Sons, Inc., 111 River St., Hoboken, NJ 07030, (201) 748-6011, fax (201) 748-6008, www.wiley.com/go/permissions.

Microfilm copies of issues and articles are available in 16 mm and 35 mm, as well as microfiche in 105 mm, through University Microfilms, Inc., 300 North Zeeb Road, Ann Arbor, Michigan 48106-1346.

ISSN 1520-3247   electronic ISSN 1534-8687

NEW DIRECTIONS FOR CHILD AND ADOLESCENT DEVELOPMENT is part of The Jossey-Bass Education Series and is published quarterly by Wiley Subscription Services, Inc., a Wiley company, at Jossey-Bass, One Montgomery Street, Suite 1200, San Francisco, CA 94104-4594. Postmaster: Send address changes to New Directions for Child and Adolescent Development, Jossey-Bass, One Montgomery Street, Suite 1200, San Francisco, CA 94104-4594.

New Directions for Child and Adolescent Development is indexed in Cambridge Scientific Abstracts (CSA/CIG), CHID: Combined Health Information Database (NIH), Contents Pages in Education (T&F), Educational Research Abstracts Online (T&F), Embase (Elsevier), ERIC Database (Education Resources Information Center), Index Medicus/MEDLINE (NLM), Linguistics & Language Behavior Abstracts (CSA/CIG), Psychological Abstracts/PsycINFO (APA), Social Services Abstracts (CSA/CIG), SocINDEX (EBSCO), and Sociological Abstracts (CSA/CIG).

INDIVIDUAL SUBSCRIPTION RATE (in USD): $89 per year US/Can/Mex, $113 rest of world; institutional subscription rate: $416 US, $456 Can/Mex, $490 rest of world. Single copy rate: $29. Electronic only–all regions: $89 individual, $416 institutional; Print & Electronic–US: $98 individual, $500 institutional; Print & Electronic–Canada/Mexico: $98 individual, $540 institutional; Print & Electronic–Rest of World: $122 individual, $574 institutional.

COVER PHOTOGRAPHS: ©iStock.com/paulaphoto (top); ©iStock.com/vm (middle); ©iStock.com/ericsphotography (bottom).

EDITORIAL CORRESPONDENCE should be e-mailed to the editors-in-chief: Lene Arnett Jensen (ljensen@clarku.edu) and Reed W. Larson (larsonr@illinois.edu).

Jossey-Bass Web address: www.josseybass.com

Contents

1. Some Long-Standing and Emerging Research Lines in Africa   1
Robert Serpell, Kofi Marfo
The authors contend that early debates about the generalizability of Western theories of child development should give way to a focus on responding to developmental phenomena distinctive to the African region.

2. Biomedical Risk, Psychosocial Influences, and Developmental Outcomes: Lessons From the Pediatric HIV Population in Africa   23
Amina Abubakar
The author reviews evidence that the impact of HIV and AIDS on child development in Africa involves interaction between biological and psychosocial factors, and outlines strategies of quantitative analysis to determine causal pathways as a guide to pediatric intervention.

3. African Early Childhood Development Curriculum and Pedagogy for Turkana Nomadic Pastoralist Communities of Kenya   43
John T. Ng'asike
The author critiques the current early childhood educational provision for a pastoralist community in Kenya and proposes a framework for integrating indigenous knowledge and ecoculturally prevalent learning contexts into ECE instructional programs.

4. Promoting Children's Sustainable Access to Early Schooling in Africa: Reflections on the Roles of Parents in Their Children's Early Childhood Care and Education   61
Jacob Marriote Ngwaru
The author reviews his research in rural Zimbabwe, Kenya, Uganda, and Tanzania showing that support for children's transition from home to school suffers from weak parental participation and lack of appropriate learning materials, and advocates for more culturally responsive early childhood education.

5. Design and Validation of Assessment Tests for Young Children in Zambia   77
Beatrice Matafwali, Robert Serpell
The authors explain the need for culturally appropriate child assessment instruments and describe two programs of test development in Zambia.

6. Some Growth Points in African Child Development 97
Research
Robert Serpell, Kofi Marfo
The editors present concluding observations and perspectives on how
the invited authors respond to key challenges identified by the editors
and, in so doing, help advance an African field of child development.

INDEX 113

Serpell, R., & Marfo, K. (2014). Some long-standing and emerging research lines in Africa. In R. Serpell & K. Marfo (Eds.), *Child development in Africa: Views from inside. New Directions for Child and Adolescent Development, 146*, 1–22.

1

Some Long-Standing and Emerging Research Lines in Africa

Robert Serpell, Kofi Marfo

Abstract

Early research on child development in Africa was dominated by expatriates and was primarily addressed to the topics of testing the cross-cultural validity of theories developed "in the West," and the search for universals. After a brief review of the outcome of that research, we propose two additional types of motivation that seem important to us as African researchers begin to take the lead in articulating research agendas for the study of child development in Africa: articulating the contextual relevance and practical usefulness of developmental psychology in Africa; and making developmental psychology intelligible to local audiences. We highlight two major challenges for African societies in this era that call for attention by the emerging field of African child development research: linguistic hegemony and its effects on research and schooling; and the process of indigenization. We end with a preview of chapters in the rest of the volume. © *2014 Wiley Periodicals, Inc.*

This volume is dedicated to showcasing research on child development in Africa by African scholars based on the continent. Researchers on child development in Africa have often originated from outside the continent, and previous commentaries have highlighted various ways in which this has colored their approach to the topic. Douglas Price-Williams (1975), Gustav Jahoda (1980), and Pierre Dasen (1977b), each of whom conducted pioneering research on aspects of child development in Africa, have all acknowledged two major types of motivation for cross-cultural research in the region: testing the cross-cultural validity of theories developed "in the West," and searching for universals. These formulations have persisted in slightly modified form in more recent reviews of the field of *cross-cultural psychology* (e.g., Berry, Poortinga, Segall, & Dasen, 2002; Segall, Dasen, Berry, & Poortinga, 1999). On the other hand, the discipline of anthropology, which informed somewhat earlier studies of African childhood (e.g., Erny, 1972; Fortes, 1938), was often motivated by a search for cross-cultural contrasts, seeking through interpretation "to make the strange familiar," and thus reflexively "to make the familiar strange" (Shweder, 1990). As Jahoda (1982) and Cole (1996) have shown, these disciplines of the Western academy emerged from common roots in the 19th century, only gradually diverged, and have since begun to converge again in the fields of cultural psychology and psychological anthropology, as well as spawning the field of *indigenous psychology* (Kim, Yang, & Hwang, 2006; Sinha, 1994, 1997).

Without contesting the relevance, nor indeed the legitimacy of any of those motivations, we propose here two additional types of motivation that seem to us important as African researchers begin to take the lead in articulating research agendas for the study of child development in Africa: (a) contextual relevance and practical usefulness, and (b) intelligibility to local audiences. We shall argue that there is a strong connection between these two goals, in that a major factor influencing the usefulness of research findings in developmental psychology is whether their interpretation connects with preoccupations of the consumers to whom it is addressed (Serpell, 1990a, 2006).

In the conclusion to his overview volume on *Psychology in Africa*, Wober (1975) urged the next generation of African social scientists to consider the possibility that they might become "more modern by not being just Western" (p. 215). The globalization of international communication has been interpreted in various ways. Some scholars see it as giving rise to increasingly egalitarian relations between nations and cultures in opportunities to define the way forward in progressive social change, due to the relatively open access to world audiences afforded by the Internet. Others, however, construe it as intensifying inequalities between powerful and less powerful sections of the world's population under the guise of universal adoption of an agenda of modernization, whose goals have been hegemonically defined by cultures originating from the former imperial and colonial powers. Depending on one's position on this continuum, responding to Wober's challenge may appear to have become more or less feasible in the four decades since it was published.

Within the field of child development, Marfo, Pence, LeVine, and LeVine (2011) reflected on why the field of African child development has been so slow to emerge. African scholarship has been constrained by the relatively late establishment of universities in most countries, by the low priority attached by the newer African universities to research, and by the tendency of many scholars to rely for their teaching on literature published outside the continent. The Marfo et al. paper arose from a meeting convened in 2009 on the theme of strengthening Africa's contributions to child development research.

A broad range of issues received attention in five other papers. Pence (2011) undertook a provocative assessment of historical events (such as colonization) and epistemological traditions that have resulted in the privileging of Western ideas and practices over non-Western ones, cautioning the early childhood development movement in Africa against uncritical adoption of so-called "best practices" from the West. One group of authors highlighted some of the major contributions to contemporary global understanding of child development generated by studies of children in Africa led and largely reported by scholars based outside the continent with the support of local, indigenous research assistants (Super, Harkness, Barry, & Zeitlin, 2011).

Serpell (2011) described a sequence of systematic inquiries between 1971 and 2008, conducted within one African country, Zambia. He observed that "the process through which this took place resembles an evolving journey rather than implementation of a preconceived blueprint" (p. 127), and that, while as lead investigator he was a long-term, cultural visitor to African cultures, "at many junctures along the way, [he] was critically supported by the co-constructive participation in research design, implementation, and interpretation by various [indigenous] African colleagues" (pp. 127–128). In a paper focusing on the application of knowledge on child development to the design and delivery of preschool programs in rural and resource-poor communities, Mwaura and Marfo (2011) traced the history of the Madrasa Preschool Resource Centers in East Africa. The paper highlighted both the adaptive application of Western program models and the challenge of depending on foreign instruments with little or no local validation to measure program outcomes.

A concluding paper by Marfo (2011) envisioned a field of "African Child Development" that addresses the most important issues within Africa's own context, particularly those dimensions of development, conceptions of development, and practices around development that are intrinsically African. As part of a global field, the African Child Development field should contribute to and benefit from conceptions and knowledge of children in other societies. It should be pluralistic in terms of research paradigms and methodologies. And it should seek to avoid some of the pitfalls identified in Western science, recognizing sociocultural diversity both across the continent and within nations, and avoiding the ethnocentric and class biases for which many studies by Western psychologists have been criticized, such as the conflation of difference with deficit. In order to build such a field, Marfo advocates the promotion of interdisciplinarity from the base of education, rather than cultivating separate disciplinary strands of expertise and then facing the challenge of integrating them. He calls for establishing African Child Development as a living, real-world field informed by a symbiotic relationship between academic researchers and professional practitioners in the community.

Motivating Trends in African Developmental Psychology

In the sections that follow, we discuss how each of the motives outlined in the previous section has influenced the character of research and dissemination about child development in Africa: testing the cross-cultural validity of theories developed "in the West," searching for universals, formulating an indigenous African psychology, attending to contextual relevance and practical usefulness, and intelligibility to local audiences. We conclude by highlighting two challenges for the field: the challenge of linguistic hegemony and its effects on education and the challenge of indigenizing child development research on the continent.

Testing the Cross-Cultural Validity of Theories Developed "in the West," and the Search for Universals. One of the widely agreed functions of scientific theory is to provide an explanation for future events that were not available at the time the theory was proposed. Generalization beyond the known is therefore an inherent feature of theories across all the disciplines. However, it is also normal to restrict the range of that generalizability when proposing a theory. The issue of what the proper limits of generalizability are for theories in developmental psychology has received considerable attention since the expansion of systematic cross-cultural research began in the 1970s.

The goal of testing the universality of a Western theoretical model was explicitly articulated by Price-Williams (1961) in a landmark study of quantitative reasoning among young children growing up in a rural African community, among the Tiv people of Central Nigeria. He concluded from his investigation that "as regards Tiv children, in the particular fields explored, there seems little difference to the sequence which has been found in European children" (p. 304). A burst of research along these lines was published by Western authors on many different African communities, as well as other "exotic" locations around the world, designed to establish whether the stages of cognitive development expounded in Piaget's "genetic epistemology" are found in societies beyond the narrow sample of Swiss children studied by Piaget and his colleagues. An early summary of the findings concluded that they confirmed Piaget's sequence of stages, from sensory-motor through egocentric/intuitive to concrete operational with no reversals of sequential order among stages; that the ages at which the transitions occur were variable across societies, and dependent on the pattern of experiences afforded by the child's eco-cultural setting, with greater susceptibility to acceleration by direct training than envisaged in the original theory; and that some societies seemingly do not promote the emergence of the final (ultimate, culminating) stage of formal operational thought (Dasen, 1972). Thus, Piaget's grand theory appeared to survive the test of relevance to African circumstances, but required the inclusion of some detailed additional parameters if it was to predict correctly the responses of African participants to the particular elicitation procedures designed by Piaget and his collaborators.

In a later review, Dasen (1977b) acknowledged some more fundamental challenges to Piagetian theory. Are there alternative developmental pathways to the same eventual end-state of formal operational thought, some of which are more compatible with particular sociocultural circumstances than others? Or is the teleological character of Piaget's sequence of stages a culturally specific feature of the theory that lacks cross-cultural validity? For instance, is the model of the child as a scientist exploring the world in search of a logically adequate explanation for its counterintuitive appearances a necessary and sufficient account of what arises as a consequence of the interaction between biological dispositions of an altricial species and the physical world in which we live and the evolutionary need to adapt in order to survive? Or is it informed by an ideological goal particular to Western society at a particular moment in history, that of achieving technological control over the physical environment? If the latter goal is related to specific sociocultural circumstances, maybe Piaget's theory is biased toward a set of goals that are neither necessary nor sufficient for healthy human development (Buck-Morss, 1975). Within Western psychology, several features of Piaget's theory came under critical examination, giving rise to a more behavioral interpretation of developmental change (Bruner, Olver, & Greenfield, 1966) than the epistemological perspective favored by Piaget. The presumption of naivete that informs Piaget's account of egocentric/intuitive thinking has been questioned in the light of dramatic increases in logical explanations generated by changing the elicitation procedures (Donaldson, 1978), and his reliance on verbal questioning has been critiqued as systematically misleading for young participants. Various neo-Piagetian models have been proposed that preserve some but not all features of the original theory. Pascual-Leone's (1976) critique of Piagetian theory's failure to take into account dynamic processes that occur within the individual during task performance and the information processing formulations of Case (1972) and Siegler (1983) brought the theory more in line with perspectives within contemporary cognitive science and also enhanced its relevance to instructional practice (e.g., Case, 1975).

Cross-cultural data, including several studies in Africa, have been invoked as significant influences on these challenges and modifications to Piaget's theory (e.g., Dasen, 1977a). Moreover, indigenous African researchers have played an ostensible and significant role in the elaboration of how the theory is best applied to the interpretation of behavioral change in Africa, both over the course of individual development and over secular time as a reflection of sociocultural processes such as education and urbanization (Adjei, 1977; Fobih, 1979; Kiminyo, 1977; Ogbonna-Ohuche & Otaala, 1981; Okonji, 1971; Owoe, 1973). Thus, the appearance of hegemonic imposition of a foreign cultural interpretation that tended to misrepresent and even sometimes to demean African cultures and societies has given way to a more reciprocally informative account of the encounter between Piaget's theory and the behavior of African children.

Witkin's theory of psychological differentiation (Witkin, Dyk, Faterson, Goodenough, & Karp, 1962) emerged from an initial focus on Gestalt principles of perception, through the elaboration of a continuum of cognitive styles (field dependency) to a broadly integrative account of how gender, culture, and socialization practices interact to generate the emergence of different patterns of personality functioning. Like Piaget's genetic epistemology, the underlying concept of psychological differentiation interprets human development from an organismic perspective. In that respect, just as the concept of stage holds together Piaget's theory, a key feature of Witkin's theory is its postulate of self-consistency across perceptual, intellectual, and socioemotional domains of personality. But, as one of its strongest African advocates observed (Okonji, 1980), cross-cultural research conducted within the framework of the theory only seldom reported evidence of intercorrelations among behaviors across that wide range of psychological domains. Moreover, while many studies claimed to support the theory "at a global level ... attempts to relate particular socialisation variables to particular modes of field approach have proved unsuccessful" (Okonji, 1980, p. 37). A sizable body of empirical research designed to test the theory's applicability across cultures was conducted in Africa in the 1960s and 1970s (e.g., Berry, 1967; Dawson, 1967; Wober, 1967), and reviewed in contrasting ways by Witkin and Berry (1975) and Serpell (1976).

An ambitious collaborative study in the 1990s sought to provide an acid test by comparing two adjacent African cultural groups in the Central African Republic, one of which, the Bangandu, a subsistence agricultural community, was theoretically chosen as likely to promote the development of a field-dependent cognitive style, while the other, the nomadic, forest-dwelling Biaka, was expected to promote field independence. Despite devoting great care to the documentation of the ecocultural niche of development afforded by each society, to the development of assessment tools, and to multivariate analysis, the study generated results so difficult to interpret that one major investigator concluded that "the hypotheses of this study were not confirmed" (van de Koppel, 1983, p. 157), while a second, multiauthored report interpreted the same data as broadly consistent with Witkin's theory and Berry's ecocultural model (Berry et al., 1988). Thus despite its meticulous attention to detail, the implications of the study are open to widely divergent interpretations (Cole, 1996; Serpell, 1990b).

The application of the developmental theories of Piaget and Witkin to the interpretation of cross-cultural variations in child behavior (notably including studies in Africa) was sharply critiqued by Cole and Scribner (1977) as providing spurious legitimation for a research agenda that was at its roots hegemonic and liable to misconstrue cross-cultural differences in cognition as manifestations of cognitive deficit and cultural deprivation in non-Western settings. The central thrust of their argument was that the focus of the theories on developmental change is intrinsically ill-suited to cross-cultural comparison, since cultural group differences are unlikely to lie along a value-laden continuum such as growth or progress. A robust defense was mounted by Dasen, Berry, and Witkin (1979) arguing, among other things, that Witkin's typology of cognitive styles was bipolar rather than a value-laden continuum. Serpell (1976), however, pointed out that the variable of field dependency was in practice most often construed as value-laden, with field-independent modes of functioning represented as more adaptive. LCHC (1982) discussed additional anomalies in the way the literature had linked field dependency to cultural variations in the African region. Okonji's (1980) profoundly reflective chapter seemed to hold out the promise of a further development of Witkin's theory in ways that would free it from such biases and generate a research program to document distinctive strengths and affordances of indigenous African sociocultural conditions as well as processes of sociocultural change. Sadly, his premature death, at age 39, in 1975 prevented him from implementing that agenda, and it does not appear to have been taken up by other researchers on the continent.

The cultural-historical perspective on human development, formulated by Vygotsky (1978) in the wake of the 1917 Russian revolution, gained widespread adoption in the field of child development since 1970, several decades after Vygotsky's death in 1934. Several American scholars expounded the theory for Western audiences, and one of these, Michael Cole, drew inspiration from it for his extensive empirical research program in Liberia in the 1960s and 1970s. A major contribution of that program was the study entitled *The Psychology of Literacy* (Scribner & Cole, 1981). This study contextualized literacy as a historically situated cultural practice and found that the cognitive outcomes of becoming literate can only be adequately explained by including a consideration of the particular characteristics of the cultural practice within which that individual literacy is deployed. Thus, rather than a general potentiating of cognition, each form of literacy *per se* conveys particular cognitive benefits, closely related to the contextual parameters of the particular practices that it mediates.

The theme of testing the cross-cultural validity of theories developed "in the West" has been represented by both the genetic epistemology camp and the psychological differentiation camp as a test of generalizability with a goal of establishing universals (Berry et al., 2002; Kagitcibasi, 2000). But critics have argued that this was a disguise, and the main lessons learned were that:

- psychological measurement is very context-dependent (Cole & Bruner, 1971; Serpell, 1979), and researchers should be wary of interpreting performance on particular tasks as evidence of broad, underlying competencies (e.g., intelligence or concrete operational reasoning) or dispositions (e.g., field-dependent cognitive style), since much of the variance in performance on those tasks is accounted for by situational variation rather than individual differences;
- a major threat to the universality of Western theories of child development was that the research strategy giving rise to them was ethnocentric (or centri-cultural). As Wober (1969) put it, what was needed was less about how well "they" can do "our [Western cultural] tricks" and more about what tricks (behavioral routines) Africans do well, why they consider them important, and how they achieve competence in them.

Serpell (1990a) argued that, in order to escape this centri-cultural constraint, studies of child development needed to

1. extend the database (observing children growing up in diverse, naturally occurring environments);
2. engage scholars with a wider range of firsthand personal developmental experiences;
3. address their interpretations to a wider range of stakeholders around the world.

In the African context, these stipulations pose three challenges: contextual diversity, reflexivity, and intelligibility and relevance to local audiences. These challenges intersect within the concept of the developmental niche (Super & Harkness, 1986) as a mandate to investigate child development in a variety of settings/ecocultural contexts, examining a variety of cultural customs, practices, and traditions, and including as theoretical resources a variety of cultural meaning systems (including languages).

Articulating the Contextual Relevance and Practical Usefulness of Developmental Psychology in Africa. Most of Africa's universities were established in the 1950s and 1960s around the end of the colonial period. Embedded in the larger vision that governments of newly independent nations had for their emerging universities was the value of contextual relevance. Throughout the continent, parliamentary acts and leadership speeches inaugurating the new institutions conveyed the imperative for them to be contextually relevant. For instance, President Nyerere of Tanzania in 1966 underscored the *local development* value of the university in these words quoted by Coleman and Court (1993):

> The university in a developing country must put the emphasis of its work on subjects of immediate moment to the nation in which it exists, and it must be committed to the people of that nation and their humanistic goals ... We in poor societies can only justify expenditure on a University—of any type—if it promotes real development of our people. (p. 296)

At its 1969 conference in Kinshasa, the newly formed Association of African Universities (AAU) characterized African universities as institutions "that are not only built, owned and sited in Africa, but are of Africa, drawing their inspiration from Africa, and intelligently dedicated to her ideas and aspirations"—institutions that will vigorously address through research "the challenges posed by the problems of poverty, and of the need for social rebirth, cultural rediscovery, and political identity, which confront African countries individually and collectively" (Yesufu, 1973, p. 5).

The emergence of African universities was part of a broader political decolonization process that famously brought a "wind of change" to the continent, one manifestation of which was the progressive replacement of expatriate professionals by indigenous Africans. Their preparation for this role in society was often conceptualized as a process of training, sometimes at a higher education institution (HEI) in a former colonial metropole, sometimes in a crash course at a newly established HEI within the continent, where the curriculum came under scrutiny for its practical usefulness and contextual relevance for professional practice in Africa. A new genre of scholarship and resource development emerged in this context, reflecting critical misgivings about the pervasive tradition of unidirectional transfer of knowledge from the Euro-American World to Africa and other parts of the Majority World.

The nurturing of children's development is a cultural project, and as such those who seek to understand children's development must understand indigenous conceptions of development—including dispositions, abilities, and behaviors at the individual and social levels—as well as the societal presuppositions and aspirations within the local context that drive what is considered at any point as valued developmental outcomes. Research on indigenous conceptions of development and quintessentially African issues emanating from them contributes both to the building of a scientific knowledge base on the continent and to a global science that benefits from alternative worldviews and conceptions of developmental phenomena across multiple cultural contexts (Marfo, 2011).

Advances in this direction are manifested in the works of an increasing number of African scholars. Since the 1970s, Serpell and his colleagues have pursued programmatic theoretical and empirical research on conceptions of intelligence in a rural Zambian community (e.g., Serpell, 1977, 1982, 1993, 2011; Serpell & Jere-Folotiya, 2008). This body of work has demonstrated that conceptions of intelligence in the rural Chewa community studied converge around two key elements—cognitive alacrity and social responsibility—both of which are valued in the local context.

Researchers in other African societies have reported congruent findings as well as additional complexities (e.g., Dasen et al., 1985; Grigorenko et al., 2001; Mpofu, 2002). This research has contributed to an appreciation of the cultural grounding of intelligence in developmental science, and in the African context, it highlights limitations of a tradition of school-driven assessment that rests exclusively on person-level cognitive and academic skills and, in so doing, short-changes education aimed at inculcating the range of competencies and dispositions necessary for children to function adaptively in school as well as community.

Earlier research on the assessment of intelligence in Africa was primarily driven by the pragmatic agenda of selecting candidates for admission to secondary and tertiary levels of formal education necessitated by the limited expansion of such provision near the end of the colonial era. Vernon (1967) justified basing selection in this context on assessment instruments originally validated in the West on the grounds that (a) "the developing countries of Africa ... want to achieve civilisations comparable to those of the Western technological nations," (b) they "are severely handicapped at present by lack of intelligent, well-educated manpower," and (c) "Western-type tests ... are known to be relevant to educational and vocational success" (p. 335). Inspired by this paternalistic rationale, the local standardization and refinement of educational selection tests became a thriving field of technical psychometric research and development in Africa during the 1960s and 1970s (e.g., Drenth, 1972; Durojaiye, 1984; Irvine, 1966), feeding the practice of importing from Western industrialized countries testing procedures that have little or no grounding in the everyday lives of most African children, outside of formal schooling (Serpell & Haynes, 2004). The divergence between the culture of schooling and that of children's homes has given rise to "a credibility gap for public basic education with respect to the values and aspirations of parents in rural communities" (Serpell, 2011, p. 128). Some attempts to move the technology of cognitive assessment in a different direction are discussed in Chapter 5 of this volume.

Making Developmental Psychology Intelligible to Local Audiences. Inquiry in the academy is often produced for consumption by fellow academics and professionals. If inquiry is to have a meaningful impact on the lives of researched communities, however, researchers have to find ways to communicate their findings in language that is comprehensible to the lay public. Horowitz (2000), in her presidential address to the Society for Research on Child Development, lamented the *de facto* practice by many academic researchers in the United States of delegating to the media the very important task of communicating research to the general public, and called on developmental scientists to also communicate their findings to "the person in the street." This responsibility takes on greater importance in the African context where communication of findings, whether to the professional or lay community, is severely constrained by a wide range of factors. Perhaps even more important, the nascence of the field in Africa makes it imperative to make communication of research to local communities a signature feature of developmental research.

The kind of orientation required to move in this direction is illustrated by Serpell's successive attempts to share the findings of his research on the indigenous conceptualization of intelligence as a dimension of child development with the rural community in Zambia's Eastern Province that hosted the research (Serpell, 1977). Over the succeeding years, following up the original child participants and their families in order to monitor developmental outcomes raised his sense of accountability to the community that had hosted more than a decade of research on the significance of schooling (Serpell, 1993). Reflecting on how best to share with them the findings of the project, the research team initially adopted a seminar format based on prevailing academic practices. Two indigenous scions of the community, who had attained tertiary level education at the national university, culled from the transcripts of interviews a collection of statements by local stakeholders about the relevance of schooling to two topics of great local salience: agriculture and health. Opposing viewpoints were selected for juxtaposition on a one-page printed document in the local language, and distributed within the village communities for perusal and reflection. Then a series of meetings were held within each village environment, and two local paraprofessionals were invited to participate: an agricultural extension officer and a clinical officer. The design of this encounter between villagers responsible for child socialization and service providers representing the national government was intended to accord legitimacy to local parents, many of whom were women, by holding the discussions in their local language and on their home territory, using their own words as the authoritative texts for discussion. Yet despite those efforts, women attending these gatherings hardly ever spoke up, leaving the floor to the menfolk, especially the government workers, who dominated the discussions and not infrequently resorted to English (the language of national power) to make their points.

Judging this first bid at generating an authentic, egalitarian discussion of the research findings to have been a failure, the research team attempted a very different strategy, inspired by a Tanzanian expert exponent of the "edutainment" form of popular theatre, Dr. Penina Mlama (1991). This time, the "text" was a drama composed collaboratively among a team of actor-musician-dramatists led by the distinguished Zambian popular theatre expert, Professor Mapopa Mtonga (2012), and a number of key informants recruited informally from among the parents, teachers, and youth who had participated in the research.

> Analysis of the informal reflections by members of the audience during and immediately following the drama showed that it had successfully engaged a wide range of local stakeholders, including women, who are a crucially important constituency both for understanding child socialization practices and for participating in the design and implementation of progressive social change. Formulating an effective dramatization of research results is at least as challenging as writing a technical paper for publication and calls for interdisciplinary collaboration. For certain important audiences, it may be the most viable way of engaging them with substantive issues identified by systematic research on African child development. (Serpell, 2011, p. 131)

The contrast between the outcomes of these two approaches to dissemination of research findings illustrates the complexity of cross-cultural communication in social science even within a single African society and among fellow citizens living in close proximity to one another. It also suggests the possibility that the most effective forms of communication may differ depending on cultural characteristics of the audience to whom they are addressed.

Challenges for Society and Field

In this final section, we identify two challenges facing African societies and, by implication, an African Child Development field. First, we explore philosophically the challenge of linguistic hegemony in post-colonial Africa and examine the practical challenge it presents for children's socialization and learning in and out of school. Second, we present perspectives on ways to think of and build an African Child Development field.

Linguistic Hegemony and Its Effects on Research and Schooling. One of the earliest explicit formulations of an indigenous psychology was by Virgilio Enriquez, who pioneered the Sikologia Pilipino movement in the 1970s that achieved remarkable prominence in the Philippines academy (Lagmay, 1984). Declaring that use of the English language had been one of the major constraints on conceptualizing psychological phenomena in ways that resonate with the indigenous culture, the movement prioritized publication of its research findings in Tagalog (also known as Pilipino). In a rare English-medium publication, Enriquez (1982) contended that significant progress had been made in articulating the interpretive power of indigenous concepts such as *saling-pusa* for an understanding of social behavior distinctive to Philippines society. In a like manner, Azuma (1984) has advanced an influential analysis of the distinctive characteristics of the Japanese concept of *amae*, which has been widely invoked to interpret distinctive features of human relationships in Japanese society (e.g., Lebra, 1994; Tobin, Wu, & Davidson, 1989).

The issue of language has yet to be systematically addressed within discussions of indigenization of psychology in Africa. The strategy of turning inward adopted by Enriquez in the Philippines has deprived the mainstream of Western psychology of the opportunity to learn from it, a concern that has also been voiced by some commentators on the decision by the distinguished African novelist and literary critic, Ngugi wa Thiongo (1986) to write exclusively in his native language, Gikuyu, after achieving fame for his earlier novels in English (e.g., Ngugi, 1964).

Schooling and the Marginalization of Indigenous Languages. At the opposite end of the pole is the marginalization of *indigenous* languages not only within formerly colonized societies, but also within contemporary industrialized societies increasingly characterized by rapid cultural change and linguistic diversity. In the United States, for example, theoretical conceptualization of how language influences child development has been constrained until quite recently by a convergence of two factors: the overwhelming dominance of the English language and an attitude toward individual bilingualism as an atypical and somewhat hazardous condition. The marginalization of other languages in the development of assessment instruments thus derived spurious justification from the political judgment that mastery of the dominant language of the state was an essential precondition for developmental success. However, the growing importance of Spanish as a language of wider communication in the United States has generated significant changes in the ways in which applied developmental science conceptualizes language as a dimension of cognition.

The empowering effects of bilingualism have been systematically documented (Bialystok, Craik, Green, & Gollan, 2009), and the rights of families to enroll their children in schools where the family's heritage language is the medium of initial literacy learning have been recognized (Cummins, 2000). The broader implications of these contextual changes have also begun to receive recognition (SRCD, 2013). Despite these important advances, the dominant perspective of educational researchers in the United States and Western Europe remains grounded in an assimilationist premise: mastery of the language of the majority is posited as an essential survival goal for all children.

In formerly colonized societies, a characteristic of most contemporary African states, this premise does not have the same axiomatic status. The majority of citizens of these countries do not speak English or French as their mother tongue, nor indeed as their principal medium of everyday communication. The dominance of those formerly metropolitan languages in public affairs arises from relations of power that are undergoing a process of gradual transformation, and the emphasis on their mastery as a goal of secondary education reflects complex political and economic processes of class formation and international dependency whose sociocultural repercussions tend to outlast the structural arrangements that gave rise to them.

In post-apartheid South Africa, educational policy has boldly designated nine of the indigenous African languages as the medium of initial literacy instruction in government schools with equal status to English and Afrikaans. But the implementation of this policy faces significant challenges from the education profession and from the general public, especially with respect to the normalization of bilingualism (Banda, 2009; Heugh, 2000). Meanwhile, all across the continent, the dominance of the former metropolitan languages as media of instruction has served to constrain the publication of texts for adults and for children in the indigenous African languages (Edwards & Ngwaru, 2011). This has in turn tended to stunt the literary development of those languages.

Most African languages were first committed to writing in the 19th or 20th century by Christian missionaries, whose choice of orthographic conventions was strongly influenced by the spelling system of their original mother tongue and/or of the European language of colonial administration, giving rise in the post-colonial era to many anomalies with respect to standardization, and to gratuitous impediments to mutual intelligibility among cognate local languages and dialects within the region (Banda, 2008). In Zambia, recent moves by the national government (GRZ, 2013) to intensify implementation of its 1996 decision to provide initial literacy instruction to all children in a familiar language point to the likelihood of a resurgence of writing and publication for children in the African languages, and with that a more effective mobilization of the widely acknowledged African cultural resource of narratives (Cancel, 2013). An African field of child development can contribute significant insights on (a) the manner in which imposed foreign languages affect children's development and learning and (b) the degree to which policies advancing the use of local languages in school might rectify challenges currently attributed to schooling in a predominantly foreign language learning context.

The Challenge of Indigenizing the Field. The genre of scholarship associated with the *indigenous psychology* movement (Sinha, 1997) sheds light on some of the challenges that an emerging African field faces. Kagitcibasi (2000) drew a distinction between two conceptual models: (a) an *indigenous orientation* to psychology that embraces one psychology benefiting from indigenous knowledge and (b) *indigenized psychology*, which, she contended, could result in a multiplicity of culture-specific psychologies with incompatible bodies of knowledge and, thus, preclude the search for universals. Marfo (2011), however, proposed a bridging epistemological perspective, arguing that an African field of human development should contribute to a global or unified science "in which pursuit of uniquely culture-specific understandings is not antithetical to pursuit of understandings with cross-cultural generality" (p. 143). Such a field should be "conceived not as a culturally insulated enterprise cocooned in its own traditions and designed exclusively to address questions of local relevance, but as a field that is mindful enough of the interconnectedness of the human condition across cultures to be able to benefit from and contribute to other understandings" (Marfo, 2011, p. 143).

A leading advocate of Africa-centered developmental psychology has been Bame Nsamenang, whose contributions include theoretical analysis of cultural constructs and expectations regarding human development in an African context. As backdrop to his work he invokes Mazrui's (1986) historiographical positioning of Africa's developmental landscape at the confluence of three strands of cultural heritage: one with social and cosmological traditions that are endogenous to Africa, one with origins in Islamic religion and law, and one originating from European Christian heritage, legal-administrative traditions, and scientific-technological advances. Drawing insights from the African philosophical writings of Mbiti (1969) and Moumouni (1968)—and extrapolating from child-rearing practices of the Nso of Cameroon and from parallel practices in other West African ethnic communities—Nsamenang has proposed a life-span model of "social ontogeny" that contrasts significantly with Western conceptions of social development (Nsamenang, 1992, 2006). The model delineates seven phases in the development of *social selfhood* (newborn, presocial, social novice, social entrée, social intern, adulthood, and old age), each characterized by a distinctive set of developmental tasks defined within the culture's primarily socioaffective developmental agenda. This and other contributions by Nsamenang "set the stage for normative and idiographic inquiry regarding the mechanisms of developmental change" (Marfo, 2011, p. 144).

Although many advocates of indigenous psychology appear to favor a qualitative approach, we question the presumption that pursuit of culture-specific understandings of human development requires, *ipso facto*, "holistic, qualitative, and phenomenological" methods that are more compatible with, and therefore more appropriate for, non-Western cultures (see Adair, 1999). As Marfo points out, the emergence of *cultural psychology* has refreshingly produced interpretive-qualitative frameworks that place understandings of psychological phenomena within the context of cultural meanings (e.g., Ratner, 2008; Ratner & Hui, 2003; Shweder, 1991). However, a good amount of research conducted within a cultural psychology framework employs quantitative methods as well (e.g., Cole, 1996; Greenfield, 1997). Seen in the context of mounting critiques of varying forms of hegemony (cultural, epistemological, and methodological) within Euro-American inquiry (Paul & Marfo, 2001), the emerging African field of African child development would do well to embrace methodological pluralism.

Preview of Chapters in the Rest of This Volume

In this final section, we present a brief foretaste of each of the four chapters written by cultural insiders of African societies.

Children with (or exposed to) HIV/AIDS constitute a significant proportion of children growing up in conditions of high risk in Africa. The health needs of these children and the challenges of meeting them are better known than either their developmental challenges or the prospects they have, with appropriate interventions, for optimal well-being in the cognitive, socioemotional, and academic competency domains. Scholarship on this subject makes a crucially important contribution not only to the emerging child development field on the continent but also to the knowledge base of the global field of developmental science. In Chapter 2, Amina Abubakar draws on her years of tool development and field research experience in Kenya to present a comprehensive portrait of some of the innovative research being done on the continent. In particular, she reviews and integrates empirical research findings from disparate realms of inquiry and methodological genres, and addresses a broad range of issues with significant implications for developmental interventions, conceptual analysis, and the advancement of empirical tools within the emerging field of pediatric developmental science.

The significance of early childhood development/education continues to gain global attention, with significant increases in investments by international donor agencies to encourage national governments in low- and middle-income countries to develop and implement policies to give all children a strong start in life. Accompanying the widespread appeal of these global investments, however, are deep concerns, within the Majority World, about the service delivery models and program content being promoted globally.

In Chapter 3, John T. Ng'asike goes beyond these program-level concerns to explore fundamental issues of profound epistemological and ontological importance for the African child development field. Using his native Turkana pastoralist cultural heritage as a case study, Ng'asike presents a penetrating critique of the content and methods of official early childhood developmental and educational programs in Kenya. The chapter provides insights into the daily lives of children in pastoralist communities, underscores how developmental and learning processes in the community context are at variance with the content and pedagogy of official Early Childhood Education, and presents a *reconceptualist* case for rethinking Early Childhood Education in the African context.

The home setting is the earliest context for children's acquisition of the competencies and dispositions that will define their readiness to enter and do well in school. The home is itself nested in the larger community and cultural context with values, resources, and knowledge traditions that shape socialization practices. A challenge in children's literacy development is that parents and significant other agents of socialization may not bring significant schooling experiences of their own to their roles as children's foundational educators. This does not mean, however, that parents and other caregivers in the lives of children do not possess valuable knowledge with direct relevance to literacy development. Marriote Ngwaru brings to the analysis of contextual issues in literacy development the benefit of his research in Kenya, Tanzania, Uganda, and Zimbabwe. Ngwaru foregrounds issues of parental involvement and empowerment in his discussion, placing them in juxtaposition to parents' own conceptions of what they bring to their children's literacy development and to a tradition of schooling in which the sociocultural funds of knowledge within local communities are often discounted, if not disregarded outright.

Assessment, whether for diagnostic and intervention purposes or for research designed to gain basic understandings about psychological and educational phenomena, remains one of the most vexing problems in the field of human development globally. In the North American context, the persistent use of assessment tools outside populations for which they were validated has been criticized (e.g., Betancourt & Lopez, 1993) and blamed in part on the culture gap in the developmental science knowledge base (Marfo & Boothby, 1997). In the African context, the preponderant dependence on assessment tools developed and validated outside the continent is even more profoundly problematic. In Chapter 5, Beatrice Matafwali and Robert Serpell address multiple dimensions of this problem. Beyond critique of the *status quo*, the authors highlight and offer perspectives on issues pertinent to the development of instruments appropriate for the African context. The insights and recommendations Matafwali and Serpell present in the chapter are informed by test design research projects in Zambia with which they have had varying levels of involvement in recent years.

In our concluding chapter, we reflect on some key insights presented in the four invited chapters, and, drawing on some of the broader themes addressed in the present chapter, we outline what appear to us important growth points of the emerging program of research initiated by this volume's sample of the current generation of African scholars studying African children within the African continent.

References

Adair, J. G. (1999). Indigenization of psychology: The concept and its practical implementation. *Applied Psychology: An International Review, 48*, 403–418.

Adjei, K. (1977). Influence of specific maternal occupation and behaviour on Piagetian cognitive development. In P. R. Dasen (Ed.), *Piagetian psychology: Cross-cultural contributions* (pp. 227–256). New York, NY: Gardner Press.

Azuma, H. (1984). Psychology in a non-Western country. *International Journal of Psychology, 19*, 45–55.

Banda, F. (2008). Orthography design and harmonization in development in Southern Africa. *Open Space, 2*(3), 39–48.

Banda, F. (2009). Critical perspectives on language planning and policy in Africa: Accounting for the notion of multilingualism. *Stellenbosch Papers in Linguistics, PLUS, 38*, 1–11.

Berry, J. W. (1967). Independence and conformity in subsistence-level societies. *Journal of Personality and Social Psychology, 7*, 415–418.

Berry, J. W., Poortinga, Y. H., Segall, M. H., & Dasen, P. R. (2002). *Cross-cultural psychology: Research and applications* (2nd Rev. ed.). Cambridge, UK: Cambridge University Press.

Berry, J. W., van de Koppel, J. M. H., Annis, R. C., Senechal, C., Bahuchet, S., Cavalli-Sforza, L. L., & Witkin, H. A. (1988). *On the edge of the forest: Cultural adaptation and cognitive development in Central Africa*. Lisse, The Netherlands: Swets & Zeitlinger.

Betancourt, H., & Lopez, S. R. (1993). The study of culture, ethnicity, and race in American psychology. *American Psychologist, 48*, 629–637.

Bialystok, E., Craik, F. I. M., Green, D. W., & Gollan, T. H. (2009). Bilingual minds. *Psychological Science: In the Public Interest, 10*(3), 89–129.

Bruner, J. S., Olver, R. R., & Greenfield, P. M. (1966). *Studies in cognitive growth*. New York, NY: Wiley.

Buck-Morss, S. (1975). Socio-economic bias in Piaget's theory and its implications for cross-cultural studies. *Human Development, 18*, 35–49.

Cancel, R. (2013). *Storytelling in Northern Zambia: Theory, method, practice and other necessary fictions*. Cambridge, UK: Open Books.

Case, R. (1972). Learning and development: A neo-Piagetian interpretation. *Human Development, 15*, 339–358.

Case, R. (1975). Gearing the demands of instruction to the developmental capacities of the learner. *Review of Educational Research, 45*, 59–87.

Cole, M. (1996). *Cultural psychology: A once and future discipline*. Cambridge, MA: Harvard University Belknap Press.

Cole, M., & Bruner, J. S. (1971). Cultural differences and inferences about psychological processes. *American Psychologist, 26*, 867–876.

Cole, M., & Scribner, S. (1977). Developmental theories applied to cross-cultural cognitive research. *Annals of the New York Academy of Sciences, 285*, 366–373.

Coleman, J. S., & Court, D. (1993). *University development in the Third World: The Rockefeller Foundation experience*. New York, NY: Pergamon Press.

Cummins, J. (2000). *Language, power, and pedagogy: Bilingual children in the crossfire*. Clevedon, UK: Multilingual Matters.

Dasen, P. R. (1972). Cross-cultural Piagetian research: A summary. *Journal of Cross-Cultural Psychology, 3*(1), 23–40.

Dasen, P. R. (1977a). Are cognitive processes universal? A contribution to cross-cultural Piagetian psychology. *Studies in Cross-Cultural Psychology, 1*, 155–201.

Dasen, P. R. (1977b). *Piagetian psychology: Cross-cultural contributions*. New York, NY: Gardner (Halsted/Wiley).

Dasen, P. R., Barthelemy, D., Kan, E., Kouame, K., Daouda, K., Adjei, K. K., & Assande, N. (1985). N'Glouele, l'intelligence chez les Baoule. *Archives de Psychologie, 53*, 295–324.

Dasen, P. R., Berry, J. W., & Witkin, H. A. (1979). The use of developmental theories cross-culturally. In L. Eckensberger, Y. Poortinga, & W. Lonner (Eds.), *Cross-cultural contributions to psychology* (pp. 69–82). Amsterdam, The Netherlands: Swets & Zeitlinger.

Dawson, J. L. M. (1967). Cultural and physiological influences on spatial-perceptual processes in West Africa, Part II. *International Journal of Psychology, 2*, 171–185.

Donaldson, M. (1978). *Children's minds*. London, UK: Fontana.

Drenth, P. J. D. (1972). Implications of testing for individual and society. In L. J. Cronbach & P. J. D. Drenth (Eds.), *Mental tests and cultural adaptation* (pp. 23–26). The Hague, The Netherlands: Mouton.

Durojaiye, M. O. A. (1984). The impact of psychological testing on educational and personnel selection in Africa. *International Journal of Psychology, 19*, 135–144.

Edwards, V., & Ngwaru, J. M. (2011). Multilingual education in South Africa: The role of publishers. *Journal of Multilingual and Multicultural Development, 32*, 435–450.

Enriquez, V. G. (1982). *Towards a Filipino psychology: Essays and studies on language and culture*. Quezon City, Philippines: Psychology Research and Training House.

Erny, P. (1972). *L'enfant et son milieu en Afrique noire*. Paris, France: Payot. (cf. English translation by Wanjohi)

Fobih, D. K. (1979). *The influence of different educational experiences on classificatory and verbal reasoning behaviour in children in Ghana* (Unpublished doctoral dissertation). University of Alberta, Edmonton, Canada.

Fortes, M. (1938). Social and psychological aspects of education in Taleland. *Africa*, *11*(Suppl.), 1–64.

Government of the Republic of Zambia (GRZ). (2013). *National Literacy Framework*. Lusaka, Zambia: Ministry of Education, Science, Vocational Training and Early Education.

Greenfield, P. M. (1997). You can't take it with you: Why ability assessments don't cross cultures. *American Psychologist*, *52*, 1115–1124.

Grigorenko, E. L., Geissler, P. W., Prince, R., Okatcha, F., Nokes, C., Kenny, D. A., ... Sternberg, R. J. (2001). The organization of Luo conceptions of intelligence: A study of implicit theories in a Kenyan village. *International Journal of Behavioral Development*, *25*, 367–378.

Heugh, K. (2000). *The case against bilingual & multilingual education in South Africa*. PRAESA Occasional Papers. Retrieved from http://www.praesa.org.za/files/2012/07/Paper6.pdf

Horowitz, F. D. (2000). Child development and the PITS: Simple questions, complex answers, and developmental theory. *Child Development*, *71*, 1–10.

Irvine, S. H. (1966). Towards a rationale for testing attainments and abilities in Africa. *British Journal of Educational Psychology*, *36*, 24–32.

Jahoda, G. (1980). Theoretical and systematic approaches in cross-cultural psychology. In H. Triandis & W. Lambert (Eds.), *Handbook of cross-cultural psychology* (Vol. 1, pp. 69–141). Boston, MA: Allyn & Bacon.

Jahoda, G. (1982). *Psychology and anthropology: A psychological perspective*. London, UK: Academic Press.

Kagitcibasi, C. (2000). Indigenous psychology and indigenous approaches to developmental research. *Newsletter of the Society for the Study of Behavioral Development*, *1* (Serial No. 37), 6–9.

Kim, U., Yang, K. S., & Hwang, K. K. (Eds.). (2006). *Indigenous and cultural psychology: Understanding people in context*. New York, NY: Springer.

Kiminyo, D. M. (1977). Is the rate of cognitive development uniform across cultures? A methodological critique with new evidence from Temne children. In P. R. Dasen (Ed.), *Piagetian psychology: Cross-cultural contributions* (pp. 26–63). New York, NY: Gardner Press.

Lagmay, A. V. (1984). Western psychology in the Philippines: impact and response. *International Journal of Psychology*, *19*(1–4), 31–44.

LCHC. (1982). Culture and intelligence. In R. J. Sternberg (Ed.), *Handbook of human intelligence* (pp. 642–719). Cambridge, UK: Cambridge University Press.

Lebra, T. S. (1994). Mother and child in Japanese socialisation: A Japan–U.S. comparison. In P. M. Greenfield & R. R. Cocking (Eds.), *Cross-cultural roots of minority child development* (pp. 259–274). Hillsdale, NJ: Erlbaum.

Marfo, K. (2011). Envisioning an African child development field. *Child Development Perspectives*, *5*, 140–147.

Marfo, K., & Boothby, L. (1997). The behavioural sciences and special education research: Some promising directions and challenging legacies. In J. L. Paul, M. Churton, H. Rosselli-Kostoryz, W. C. Morse et al. (Eds.), *Foundations of special education: Basic knowledge informing research and practice in special education* (pp. 247–278). Pacific Grove, CA: Brooks/Cole.

Marfo, K., Pence, A. R., LeVine, R. A., & LeVine, S. (2011). Introduction to the special section: Strengthening Africa's contributions to child development research. *Child Development Perspectives, 5*, 104–111.
Mazrui, A. (1986). *The Africans.* New York, NY: Praeger.
Mbiti, J. S. (1969). *African religions and philosophy.* London, UK: Heinemann.
Mlama, P. (1991). *Culture and development: The popular theatre approach in Africa.* Uppsala, Sweden: Nordiska Afrikainstitutet.
Moumouni, A. (1968). *Education in Africa.* London, UK: Andre Deutsch.
Mpofu, E. (2002). Indigenization of the psychology of human intelligence in Sub-Saharan Africa. *Online Readings in Psychology and Culture, Unit 4.* Retrieved from http://scholarworks.gvsu.edu/orpc/vol4/iss3/2
Mtonga, M. (2012). *Children's games and play in Zambia.* Lusaka, Zambia: University of Zambia Press.
Mwaura, P. A. M., & Marfo, K. (2011). Bridging culture, research, and practice in early childhood development: The Madrasa Resource Centers in East Africa. *Child Development Perspectives, 5*, 134–139.
Ngugi, J. (1964). *Weep not child.* London, UK: Heinemann.
Ngugi wa Thiongo. (1986). *Decolonising the mind: The politics of language in African literature.* London, UK: Currey/Heinemann.
Nsamenang, A. B. (1992). *Human development in cultural context.* New York, NY: Russell Sage Foundation.
Nsamenang, A. B. (2006). Human ontogenesis: An indigenous African view on development and intelligence. *International Journal of Psychology, 41*, 293–297.
Ogbonna-Ohuche, R. O., & Otaala, B. (Eds.). (1981). *The African child and his environment.* Oxford, UK: Pergamon.
Okonji, M. O. (1971). The effects of familiarity on classification. *Journal of Cross-Cultural Psychology, 2*, 39–49.
Okonji, M. O. (1980). Cognitive styles across cultures. In N. Warren (Ed.), *Studies in cross-cultural psychology* (Vol. 2, pp. 1–50). London, UK: Academic Press.
Owoe, P. J. (1973). On culture and conservation once again. *International Journal of Psychology, 8*, 121–128.
Pascual-Leone, J. (1976). On learning and development, Piagetian style: II. A critical historical analysis of Geneva's research program. *Canadian Psychological Review, 17*, 289–302.
Paul, J. L., & Marfo, K. (2001). Preparation in the philosophical foundations of inquiry. *Review of Educational Research, 71*, 525–547.
Pence, A. (2011). Early childhood care and development research in Africa: Historical, conceptual, and structural challenges. *Child Development Perspectives, 5*, 112–118.
Price-Williams, D. R. (1961). A study concerning concepts of conservation of quantities among primitive children. *Acta Psychologica, 18*, 297–305.
Price-Williams, D. R. (1975). *Explorations in cross-cultural psychology.* San Francisco, CA: Chandler and Sharp.
Ratner, C. (2008). Cultural psychology and qualitative methodology: Scientific and political considerations. *Culture and Psychology, 14*, 259–288.
Ratner, C., & Hui, L. (2003). Theoretical and methodological problems in cross-cultural psychology. *Journal of the Theory of Social Behavior, 33*, 67–94.
Scribner, S., & Cole, M. (1981). *The psychology of literacy.* Cambridge, MA: Harvard University Press.
Segall, M. H., Dasen, P. R., Berry, J. W., & Poortinga, Y. H. (1999). *Human behavior in global perspective: An introduction to cross-cultural psychology* (2nd Rev. ed.). Boston, MA: Allyn & Bacon.
Serpell, R. (1976). *Culture's influence on behaviour.* London, UK: Methuen.

Serpell, R. (1977). Estimates of intelligence in a rural community of eastern Zambia. In F. M. Okatcha (Ed.), *Modern psychology and cultural adaptation* (pp. 179–216). Nairobi, Kenya: Swahili Language Consultants and Publishers.

Serpell, R. (1979). How specific are perceptual skills? A cross-cultural study of pattern recognition. *British Journal of Psychology, 70,* 365–380.

Serpell, R. (1982). Measures of perception, skills, and intelligence: The growth of a new perspective on children in a Third World country. In W. W. Hartup (Ed.), *Review of Child Development Research* (Vol. 6, pp. 392–440). Chicago, IL: University of Chicago Press.

Serpell, R. (1990a). Audience, culture and psychological explanation: A reformulation of the emic-etic problem in cross-cultural psychology. *Quarterly Newsletter of the Laboratory of Comparative Human Cognition, 12*(3), 99–132. Retrieved from http://lchc.ucsd.edu/Histarch/newsletters.html

Serpell, R. (1990b). Book review of Berry et al. On the Edge of the Forest. *Journal of Cross-Cultural Psychology, 21,* 119–121.

Serpell, R. (1993). *The significance of schooling: Life-journeys in an African society.* Cambridge, UK: Cambridge University Press.

Serpell, R. (2006). Negotiating the middle ground between the ostensible and shared horizons: A dynamic approach to cross-cultural communication about human development. In J. Straub, D. Weidemann, C. Kölbl, & B. Zielke (Eds.), *Pursuit of meaning: Advances in cultural and cross-cultural psychology* (pp. 393–433). Berlin, Germany: Verlag.

Serpell, R. (2011). Social responsibility as a dimension of intelligence, and as an educational goal: Insights from programmatic research in an African society. *Child Development Perspectives, 5,* 126–133.

Serpell, R., & Haynes, B. (2004). The cultural practice of intelligence testing: Problems of international export. In R. J. Sternberg & E. Grigorenko (Eds.), *Culture and competence: Contexts of life success* (pp. 163–185). Washington, DC: American Psychological Association.

Serpell, R., & Jere-Folotiya, J. (2008). Developmental assessment, cultural context, gender and schooling in Zambia. *International Journal of Psychology, 43,* 88–96.

Shweder, R. A. (1990). Cultural psychology—What is it? In J. W. Stigler, R. A. Shweder, & G. Herdt (Eds.), *Cultural psychology: Essays on comparative human development* (pp. 1–43). Cambridge, UK: Cambridge University Press.

Shweder, R. A. (1991). *Thinking through cultures: Expeditions in cultural psychology.* Cambridge, MA: Harvard University Press.

Siegler, R. S. (1983). Information processing approaches to development. In P. Mussen (Ed.), *Handbook of child psychology* (pp. 129–211). New York, NY: Wiley.

Sinha, D. (1994). Indigenous psychology: Need and potentiality. *Journal of Indian Psychology, 12,* 1–7.

Sinha, D. (1997). Indigenizing psychology. In J. W. Berry, Y. H. Poortinga, & J. M. Pandey (Eds.), *Handbook of cross-cultural psychology, Volume 1: Theory and Method* (2nd ed., pp. 129–169). Boston, MA: Allyn & Bacon.

SRCD. (2013). *Ensuring that multilingual children benefit from best practices* (Policy Brief No. 27(4): sharing child and youth development knowledge). Retrieved from http://www.srcd.org/sites/default/files/documents/washington/spr_brief_2014_04_09_multilingualchildren.pdf

Super, C. M., & Harkness, S. (1986). The developmental niche: A conceptualization at the interface of child and culture. *International Journal of Behavioral Development, 9,* 515–569.

Super, C. M., Harkness, S., Barry, O., & Zeitlin, M. (2011). Think locally, act globally: Contributions of African research to child development. *Child Development Perspectives, 5,* 119–125.

Tobin, J. J., Wu, D. Y. H., & Davidson, D. H. (1989). *Preschool in three cultures: Japan, China and the United States.* New Haven, CT: Yale University Press.
van de Koppel, J. M. H. (1983). *Developmental study of the Biaka Pygmies and the Bangandu.* Lisse, The Netherlands: Swets & Zeitlinger.
Vernon, P. E. (1967). Abilities and educational attainments in an East African environment. *Journal of Special Education, 1,* 335–345.
Vygotsky, L. S. (1978). *Mind in society: Development of higher psychological processes.* Cambridge, MA: Harvard University Press.
Witkin, H. A., & Berry, J. W. (1975). Psychological differentiation in cross-cultural perspective. *Journal of Cross-Cultural Psychology, 6,* 4–87.
Witkin, H. A., Dyk, R. B., Faterson, H. F., Goodenough, D. R., & Karp, S. (1962). *Psychological differentiation.* New York, NY: Wiley.
Wober, M. (1967). Adapting Witkin's field independence theory to accommodate new information from Africa. *British Journal of Psychology, 58,* 29–38.
Wober, M. (1969). Distinguishing centri-cultural from cross-cultural tests and research. *Perceptual and Motor Skills, 28,* 488.
Wober, M. (1975). *Psychology in Africa.* London, UK: International African Institute.
Yesufu, T. M. (Ed.). (1973). *Creating the African university: Emerging issues of the 1970s.* Ibadan, Nigeria: Oxford University Press.

ROBERT SERPELL *is a professor of applied developmental psychology and coordinator of the Center for Promotion of Literacy in Sub-Saharan Africa (CAPOLSA) in the School of Humanities and Social Sciences, University of Zambia.*

KOFI MARFO *is a professor and founding director of the Institute for Human Development, Aga Khan University (South-Central Asia, East Africa, and the United Kingdom), and coleader of the Africa Child Development Research Capacity Building initiative.*

Abubakar, A. (2014). Biomedical risk, psychosocial influences, and developmental outcomes: Lessons from the pediatric HIV population in Africa. In R. Serpell & K. Marfo (Eds.), *Child development in Africa: Views from inside. New Directions for Child and Adolescent Development, 146,* 23–41.

2

Biomedical Risk, Psychosocial Influences, and Developmental Outcomes: Lessons From the Pediatric HIV Population in Africa

Amina Abubakar

Abstract

Sub-Saharan Africa is home to millions of HIV-affected children. These children are likely to experience multiple developmental delays. In this chapter, I present data highlighting compromised neurobehavioral, mental health, and scholastic outcomes for children affected by HIV. Furthermore, I discuss biomedical factors (e.g., disease severity and nutritional status) that may exacerbate the adverse effects of HIV on childhood outcomes. I also present evidence on how psychosocial risk factors such as poor maternal mental health, orphanhood, and poverty may aggravate the effects of HIV. The concluding section of the chapter highlights conceptual and methodological refinements in research on the impact of HIV on child development in Sub-Saharan Africa. © 2014 Wiley Periodicals, Inc.

Early exposure to ill health places children growing up in Sub-Saharan Africa (SSA) at an elevated risk of experiencing developmental and cognitive impairments (Mwaniki, Atieno, Lawn, & Newton, 2012). Impairments associated with diseases and conditions such as HIV (Abubakar, Van Baar, Van de Vijver, Holding, & Newton, 2008), malaria (Kihara, Carter, & Newton, 2006), malnutrition (Abubakar, 2013; Walker et al., 2007), and epilepsy (Aldenkamp & Bodde, 2005) contribute to low educational achievement, to low productivity in later life, and to the vicious cycle of poverty thus perpetuating social inequalities.

Elucidating the pathways between biomedical risk and childhood outcomes can help in identifying important points of intervention. These pathways are complicated by the presence of concurrent multiple risks. Although there is a growing body of literature illustrating the interconnectedness between biomedical and psychosocial risk factors in shaping developmental outcomes, many earlier studies have only attempted to quantify the burden of disease without adequately looking at the context.

Children in Africa face a myriad of medical challenges. However, I have restricted the scope of this chapter to pediatric HIV infection, with the expectation that lessons learned from the current evidence can be applied to the study of other childhood conditions. The chapter provides a critical evaluation of the existing literature, highlighting some of the most recent works with the aim of recommending future directions. In the first section, I review the evidence base on the impact of pediatric HIV infection. The second section scours the knowledge base to demonstrate the contribution of psychosocial risk factors to poor outcomes. I conclude the chapter with recommendations for refinement of conceptual and methodological models for studies oriented toward intervention.

Biomedical Risk Factors for Poor Childhood Outcomes: Focus on HIV

Children in Africa bear a disproportionate burden of the global HIV epidemic. It is estimated that 90% (approximately 2.3 million) of all HIV-positive children worldwide live in SSA (UNAIDS, 2012). A further 16 million have been orphaned by HIV/AIDS while an estimated 70–90 million are living in families affected by parental or caregiver HIV illness (Cluver, Orkin et al., 2013).

This chapter is published with the permission of the director of KEMRI. Amina Abubakar is supported by University of Oxford Tropical Network Fund, Wellcome Trust grant 092654/Z/10/A, and the Change Fellowship (funds provided by International Union of Psychological Science, National Research Foundation, and the Jacobs Foundation). I would like to acknowledge Fons Van de Vijver, Ype Poortinga, Amin Hassan, and Patricia Kitsao-Wekulo for providing valuable feedback on an earlier version of this chapter.

HIV has a propensity to invade both the central and peripheral nervous system. Autopsies on deceased HIV-positive patients have revealed that the brain was the second most frequently affected body organ (Hardy & Vance, 2009; Sullivan, 2009; Woods, Moore, Weber, & Grant, 2009). Consequently, structural brain damage, neurological complications, and consequent neurobehavioral manifestations are common in the HIV-infected population. The broad effects of HIV on the central nervous system mean that children living with HIV face multiple developmental impairments, although these adverse effects are not universal (Sherr, Croome, Parra-Castaneda, Bradshaw, & Herrero-Romero, 2014). Here, I highlight key findings and trends related to HIV-associated neurocognitive, mental health, and educational outcomes.

Neurobehavioral Outcomes. Childhood HIV has been related to adverse outcomes in motor, language, and cognitive domains (referred to here together as neurobehavioral outcomes). Studies of HIV-infected infants in Africa report impairments in motor, mental, and neurological functioning in the first two years of life (Drotar et al., 1997; Msellati et al., 1993). Multiple developmental delays have also been observed among preschool children. For instance, Van Rie, Mupuala, and Dow (2008), working in the Democratic Republic of Congo, observed that HIV-positive children suffered motor, language, and cognitive deficits. In a study involving 37 HIV-infected, 35 HIV-affected (see "Uninfected Children of HIV-Infected Parents" section), and 90 control children aged 18–72 months, it was observed that 60% of HIV-infected children had severe delay in cognitive function, 29% had severe delay in motor skills, 85% had delay in language expression, and 77% had delay in language comprehension, all at significantly higher rates compared with the control children. With one exception (Bagenda et al., 2006), all identified studies investigating neurocognitive outcomes among school-going children have observed delays (see Boivin et al., 2010; Ruel et al., 2012; Smith, Adnams, & Eley, 2008). The overall pattern of results indicates that children infected with HIV experience multiple developmental impairments early in life, and these impairments persist into late childhood and later life. Table 2.1 provides a summary of all the data that I was able to find on neurobehavioral outcomes of HIV infection in the African context.

Various factors may exacerbate the effects of HIV on neurobehavioral outcomes. Three of these factors that may be considered key are time of infection, disease severity, and nutritional status. In a study from Tanzania, McGrath et al. (2006) reported that children who are infected early (testing HIV positive at birth) were at a higher risk of experiencing developmental delays compared to those testing HIV-positive postnatally. Additionally, children at advanced stages of HIV infection (evaluated either by WHO disease staging or viral count) and those with poor nutritional status also performed much worse on measures of neurocognitive outcomes (Abubakar, Holding, Newton, Van Baar, & Van de Vijver, 2009; Boivin et al., 2010; Potterton et al., 2009; Ruel et al., 2012).

Table 2.1. Summary of Studies Investigating Neurocognitive Outcomes Among HIV-Infected Children in Africa

Author	Year	Country	Sample[a]	Age	ARV	Design	Tools	Key Findings	Psychosocial Aspects
Msellati et al.	1993	Rwanda	43 I, 133 E, 193 C	Birth to 24 months	No	LG	Local tool	Multiple delays. 12.5% delayed at 6 months, 20% at 18 and 9% at 24 months.	None
Boivin et al.[b]	1995	DRC	14 I, 20 E, 16 C	3–18 months	No	LG	DDST	Delays in multiple developmental domains.	None
Boivin et al.[b]	1995	DRC	11 I, 15 E, 15 C	>2 yrs	No	CS	K-ABC, ECSP	Multiple developmental delays.	None
Drotar et al.	1997, 1999	Uganda	59 I, 211 E, 107 C	Birth to 24 months	No	LG	BSID, FTII, HOME	Delays in motor and cognitive domains, none in information processing.	No difference in quality of home of HIV positive and controls
Bagenda et al.	2006	Uganda	28 I, 42 E, 37 C	6–12 years	No	CS	K-ABC, WRAT	No significant delay or impairment was reported.	None
McGrath et al.	2006	Tanzania	327 I	6–18 months	No	LG	BSID-II	Early infected performed worse than later infected.	None
Baillieu & Potterton	2008	SA	40 I	18–30 months	No	CS	BSID-II	85% gross motor and 82% language delay.	None
Smith et al.	2008	SA	39 I	14–106 months	Yes	LG	GMDS, TROG, DAP, VMI/VP/RCPM	Developmental delays observed. No change in status six months into ARV treatment.	None

(Continued)

Table 2.1. Continued

Author	Year	Country	Sample[a]	Age	ARV	Design	Tools	Key Findings	Psychosocial Aspects
Van Rie et al.	2008, 2009	DRC	35 I 35 E 90 C	18–72 months	Yes	LG	BSID-II PDMS SON	Developmental delays in infected children. After one year of medical care, HIV-infected children achieved mean motor and cognitive scores that were similar to HIV-uninfected and affected children although lower compared with control children.	None
Abubakar et al.	2009	Kenya	31 I 17 E 319 C	6–35 months	No	CS	KDI	Motor impairments. Performance worsened by disease progression and nutritional deficits.	None
Ferguson & Jelsma	2009	SA	51 I 35 C	6–32 months	34 out of 51	CS	BSID-II	66.7% of the HIV-infected children experienced motor impairments compared to 5.7% of the controls. No difference in performance between those on ARVs and those who are not.	None
Boivin et al.	2010	Uganda	102 I	6–12 years	No	CS	KABC TOVA BOT-2	HIV clade influenced neurocognitive outcome, children with subtype A performing worse than those with subtype D.	None

(Continued)

Table 2.1. Continued

Author	Year	Country	Sample[a]	Age	ARV	Design	Tools	Key Findings	Psychosocial Aspects
Kandawasvika et al.	2011	Zimbabwe	65 I 188 E 287 C	Birth to 12 months	Yes	LG	BINS	HIV-infected children twice at risk of impairment; this effect becomes nonsignificant when you take into consideration other risk factors.	Levels of family income predictive of neurodevelopmental impairments
Jelsma, Davids, & Ferguson	2011	SA	23 I 21 E	30–59 months	Yes	CS	PDMS II	Motor delays (Cohen d = 1.450).	Residence in a foster home a predictor of outcomes
Lowick, Sawry, & Meyers	2012	SA	30 I 30 E	5–6 years	Yes	CS	GMDS-R	90% of HIV-positive children and 76% of controls developmentally delayed.	None
Ruel et al.	2012	Uganda	93 I 106 E	6–12 years	No	CS	KABC TOVA BOT-2	Multiple cognitive and motor impairments. Performance worsens with advanced disease staging.	HIV positive from lower SES but same scores on HOME
Hoare et al.	2012	SA	24 I	8–12 years	No	CS	WASI Imaging	Asymptomatic HIV-positive children had poorer neurocognitive outcomes compared to controls. Indicators of imaging showed poor outcomes. Strong correlation between imaging results and neurodevelopmental outcomes.	None

(Continued)

Table 2.1. Continued

Author	Year	Country	Sample[a]	Age	ARV	Design	Tools	Key Findings	Psychosocial Aspects
Laughton et al.	2012	SA	92 I 24 E 34 C	10–16 months	Some	CS	GMDS	Children who received ARVs early performed better than those initiated to ARVs later.	None
Boyede et al.	2013a, 2013b, 2013c	Nigeria	69 I 69 E	6–15 years	56% on ARV	CS	RPM	HIV positive delayed (Cohen d of 0.76). Those on ARVs better than those not on ARVs.	SES and maternal education influenced cognitive outcomes
Whitehead et al.	2014	SA	27 I 29 E	Six months	Yes	LG	BSID-II	At baseline 48.1% cognitive impairment, 51.8% language in the HIV positive group.	None
Kandawasvika et al.	2014	Zimbabwe	32 I 121 E 153 C	6–8 years	30% on ARV	CS	MSCA	No difference in performance except on perceptual tasks.	Cognitive impairments associated with caregiver unemployment, parental loss, and undernutrition

[a]Longitudinal study, we report sample sizes at baseline.
[b]This chapter reported two different studies so we separated them in this report.
Design. LG: longitudinal; CS: cross-sectional.
Conditions. I: HIV infected; E: HIV exposed; C: community controls/HIV unexposed.
Locations. DRC: Democratic Republic of Congo formerly known as Zaire; SA: South Africa.
Instruments. DDST: Denver Developmental Screening Tool; BSID: Bayley's Scales for Infant Development; FTII: Fagan Test of Infant Intelligence; K-ABC: Kauffman Assessment Battery for Children; WRAT: Wide Range Achievement Test; KDI: Kilifi Development Inventory; GMDS-R: Griffiths Mental Developmental Scales-Revised; PDMS II: Peabody Development Motor Scale II; RPM: Raven's Progressive Matrices; BINS: Bayley Infant Neurodevelopmental Screener; TROG: Test for Reception of Grammar; DAP VMI/VP/Beery-Buktenica developmental tests for visual motor integration (VMI), visual perception (VP), and motor coordination (MC); MSCA: McCarthy Scales of Children's Abilities.

The use of antiretrovirals (ARVs) improves clinical, immunological, and nutritional outcomes, leading to a significant decrease in mortality among infected children (Kabue et al., 2012). However, especially within the African context, there is limited evidence of the benefits of ARV use on neurobehavioral functioning. Results from the few studies in Africa examining the neurobehavioral impact of ARVs have not been consistent (see Table 2.1 for the pattern of results). The lack of positive effects may be related to various factors such as timing of treatment initiation and the lack of properly designed studies to investigate the impact of treatment. For instance, a study in South Africa involving 29 HIV-infected infants observed that the children on ARVs did not show improvement in their neurodevelopmental outcomes after initiation of treatment. However, they also did not show deterioration, something that was common in the pre-ARV use period (Whitehead, Potterton, & Coovadia, 2014). The authors concluded that their results could indicate that ARVs can stop further neurological damage, but may be unable to reverse the neurological damage experienced prior to treatment. The use of cross-sectional data or very short-term longitudinal data in the African-based studies on the neurocognitive outcomes of childhood HIV infection is a major limitation. As a result, little is known of developmental trajectories or of the long-term impact of treatment.

Mental Health. Research evidence on the social, emotional, and behavioral outcomes associated with being HIV positive during infancy and early childhood is scant, especially in the African context. Early work by scholars such as Msellati et al. (1993) and Boivin et al. (1995) has already documented impairments among HIV-positive children in their social and emotional functioning. Among older children the issue of mental health has been studied in greater detail. Here, mixed results have been reported, with some studies indicating poor outcomes while others did not observe any adverse effects of HIV. In an initial report, Menon, Glazebrook, Campain, and Ngoma (2007) looked at mental health outcomes of 127 HIV-infected adolescents from Zambia. They administered the Strengths and Difficulties Questionnaire (SDQ; Goodman, 1997) and compared data from Zambia to British norms. Results indicated that the HIV-positive Zambian adolescents were at greater risk of mental health problems compared to the British sample. However, these comparisons should be made with caution as earlier cross-cultural studies discourage the use of norms from a different culture without adequately evaluating their validity. In subsequent reanalysis, Menon, Glazebrook, and Ngoma (2009) compared the data from the HIV-positive adolescents to a large sample of adolescents recruited from five Zambian high schools ($N = 702$). The study observed that while the Zambian adolescents (both infected and uninfected) had higher scores on the SDQ compared to the British sample, affected and unaffected adolescents did not significantly differ from each other. This finding suggested that HIV-positive adolescents did not experience more mental health problems than their uninfected peers. In another study from Uganda, Musisi and Kinyanda (2009) reported high rates of psychiatric problems among HIV-positive adolescents. In their study, they found that 51.2% of the subjects had significant psychological distress (Self-Reporting Questionnaire: 25 scores of 6 or higher) while 17.1% had attempted suicide within the last 12 months. A high prevalence of psychiatric problems among HIV-infected adolescents has also been reported in a recent study in Kenya (Kamau, Kuria, Mathai, Atwoli, & Kangethe, 2012) in which 48% of the adolescents presented with psychiatric morbidity. This rate was much higher than the observed 20% in the general population. It must be noted, however, that the comparison figure was based on data collected more than 20 years ago, while the HIV data were more recent.

Various methodological shortfalls make it difficult to draw firm conclusions on the prevalence of mental health problems among HIV-infected children and adolescents in the African context. Such limitations include the use of measures not validated in context, with resultant poor psychometric properties. For instance, Menon et al. (2007) used the SDQ which yielded very low reliability levels (alphas ranging from 0.18 to 0.55) in the Zambian population. In addition, these studies did not control for potentially confounding factors (e.g., use of ARVs, home environment, and caregiver characteristics). Moreover, the lack of norms on mental health outcomes in the African context requires that studies be designed with carefully defined controls in order to adequately estimate the additional risk that being HIV-infected presents. There is a need for studies investigating the etiology, correlates, and patterns of mental health outcomes in children living with HIV.

Educational Outcomes. Relatively little is known of the educational outcomes of HIV-infected children. In one of the earliest studies of school-aged children, Bagenda et al. (2006) found no differences in achievement test scores between infected pupils and controls. However, a recent study by Devendra, Makawa, Kazembe, Calles, and Kuper (2013) in Malawi reported that HIV-infected children were more frequently absent from school, less likely to be in the appropriate grade level for their age, and less likely to achieve "above-average" school grades compared to their uninfected siblings. In a Kenyan study, Kamau et al. (2012) noted that 49% of the HIV-infected adolescents in their sample were at least two grades behind their peers. There is a need to carry out extensive investigations of the impact of perinatal HIV infection on educational outcomes.

Uninfected Children of HIV-Infected Parents

This group refers to children who were exposed to HIV prenatally, through maternal HIV infection, children for whom one or both parents is living with HIV, or children orphaned by an HIV-related illness. I refer to them as HIV-affected children. These children have been observed to experience various developmental delays, especially in the African context (Le Doaré, Bland, & Newell, 2012). Two potential pathways that may contribute to these delays have been hypothesized. The first is prenatal and early postnatal exposure to biomedical risk factors (Filteau, 2009). The second is the environmentally or socially mediated effect of growing up in a family affected by HIV. Children of parents who are HIV positive experience multiple stressors, such as parental illness and death, suboptimal parenting behaviors, stigma, destabilized home environment, and poor nutritional status (see Filteau, 2009, for a more detailed analysis of this issue). Given these circumstances, it is not surprising that studies in Africa report neurocognitive delays (Le Doaré et al., 2012), mental health problems (Cluver & Gardner, 2006; Cluver, Gardner, & Operario, 2007), and poor educational outcomes (Guo, Li, & Sherr, 2012) for HIV-affected children.

HIV-affected children form the largest group of children adversely affected by the HIV pandemic. Understanding factors that put them at risk of poor developmental outcomes will inform the design of effective services aimed at enhancing their quality of life. Moreover, as this group shares the environmental risk experienced by HIV-infected children, they form an important control group for a study seeking to disentangle the associations between biomedical and psychosocial risk factors. Carefully designed studies comparing HIV-infected and HIV-affected children will go a long way in helping us understand the relative contribution of co-occurring risk factors.

The Clustering of Risk Factors

Worldwide, many children infected or affected by HIV are exposed to multiple risk environments—poverty, multiple losses through death, maternal depression, stigma, and suboptimal parenting behavior—all of which contribute to poor outcomes independent of HIV status (Stein et al., 2005). In the next section, I discuss some of the most salient risk factors that impact child development in the context of HIV.

Poverty. The relationship between socioeconomic status (SES) and HIV in Africa is not straightforward. HIV infection is by no means a disease of the poor. However, parental HIV infection may be related to poverty in various ways. First, parental HIV infection is likely to lead to prolonged periods of illness, lowered productivity, and extra medical-related expenses, contributing to lowered economic status for the family. Second, with improved treatment and care, HIV has changed from a fatal illness into a chronic one. A proper treatment regimen requires medication and adequate nutrition, among other factors. In extreme poverty situations, the lack of money to buy food or medication may exacerbate poor outcomes for children of people living with HIV, above and beyond the impact of HIV. Third, the environment of poverty, with the concomitant lack of clean water, poor hygiene, inadequate sanitation coupled with overcrowding, implies a higher risk of exposure to pathogens which increases the ease with which one is infected with opportunistic diseases. The resultant poor health in the infected parents contributes to suboptimal child development.

Maternal Psychosocial Functioning. Research indicates that people living with HIV are at a higher risk of poor mental health outcomes. For instance, Seth et al. (2014) in a study across three countries (Tanzania, Kenya, and Namibia) observed that up to 27% of the people living with HIV reported mild to severe depressive symptoms. The literature reveals that maternal mental health problems are likely to impact parenting behavior adversely, which in turn results in poor child function. A study involving 361 mother–child dyads in Tshwane, South Africa (Allen et al., 2014), investigated the relationships among mothers' psychological functioning, parenting behavior, and children's behavioral outcomes. The children were aged between 6 and 10 years. Using path analytic approaches, the authors reported that maternal depression was related to an increase in parenting stress and dysfunction in parent–child interactions, which in turn was associated with increased behavioral and emotional problems in children. The negative impact of compromised maternal psychosocial function within the context of HIV has also been reported among HIV-infected children. In a study of 119 children aged 1–5 years, Busman, Page, Oka, Giordani, and Boivin (2013) observed the caregiving context and found that the quality of the home environment was associated with externalizing behavioral problems among HIV-positive children.

Orphanhood. HIV-related orphanhood contributes to poor developmental, educational, and mental health outcomes. A study in Kenya involving 325 adolescents found that orphans experienced poorer mental health, had less social support, and fewer material resources (Puffer et al., 2012). Unfortunately, as the negative effects of HIV orphanhood are not transient, mental health conditions of HIV-orphaned children continue to be compromised as demonstrated through follow-up studies. A four-year longitudinal study of 1,021 South African children showed that AIDS-orphaned children had higher depression, anxiety, and posttraumatic stress disorder (PTSD) scores at both baseline and follow-up when compared with nonorphans and children orphaned through other reasons (Cluver, Orkin, Gardner, & Boyes, 2012). These effects remained even after controlling for background factors such as SES and age.

Stigma. HIV-related stigma is highly prevalent in many African countries and is experienced in various forms including abuse, discrimination, and exclusion. In a longitudinal study covering five African countries, up to 84% of people living with HIV reported having experienced at least one stigmatizing event in the past one year at baseline (Holzemer et al., 2009). At the 12-month follow-up, this figure declined to 65%, still considered a very high percentage. In the same study, up to 80% of nurses had observed at least one stigmatizing event against HIV-positive patients during the past one year; this figure increased to 84% during the follow-up period (12 months later; Holzemer et al., 2009).

HIV-related stigma adversely influences the quality of life of people living with HIV (Herrmann et al., 2013; Li et al., 2011). It also limits participation in social, economic, and cultural activities, as well as access to health services. These factors are likely to lead to suboptimal parenting behavior for adults who are parents, resulting in adverse outcomes for their children. Thus, parental perceived or experienced stigma has a negative influence on child adjustment.

Stigma affects HIV-infected and HIV-affected children both directly and indirectly. For instance, Boyes and Cluver (2013) reported higher levels of perceived stigma, anxiety, and depression among HIV/AIDS orphans. The results of a path analysis showed that orphanhood was not directly related to poor mental health; rather, stigma mediated the relationship between orphanhood and psychological adjustment. The indirect effects of stigma on child development are seen in the manner in which parental stigma impacts parental childrearing abilities.

In summary, children who are HIV infected or affected experience developmental delays which may be related to biomedical, psychosocial risk factors, or a combination. How do we intervene to enhance psychosocial development and quality of life most effectively? Which are the most meaningful points of intervention? Where can we make the most impact to ensure that HIV-infected and HIV-affected children do *not just survive but thrive*? The available evidence provides a lot of information but major gaps still exist. Further refinement of both conceptual and methodological approaches will ensure that a strong evidence base guides intervention.

Future Directions

Compared with the literature from other parts of the world which carry a smaller disease burden, the study of the effects of pediatric HIV in Africa is relatively limited. Nevertheless, there are many important lessons to be learned. From the literature reviewed here, it is evident that we have gathered knowledge on the effects of HIV on various domains, on the biomedical factors that contribute to these adverse effects, and on the psychosocial influences that are likely to exacerbate the negative effects. However, current efforts on refining conceptual and methodological models should continue to guide the field in the adoption of data collection methods.

The need for this refinement arises for two reasons. First, as illustrated in Table 2.1, many studies on the impact of HIV infection on children have focused on the potential contribution of biomedical mediators (e.g., disease staging) while ignoring psychosocial issues. On the other hand, the literature on psychosocial risk has been strongly influenced by studies on HIV-affected children. There is a need for more work looking at these areas concurrently so as to gain a good understanding of factors contributing to poor outcomes in this population. Understanding factors that may contribute to poor outcomes among HIV-affected children is important since there is wide variability in outcomes, with some of these children experiencing developmental delays while others do not (Sherr et al., 2014).

Refining Conceptual Models. As earlier noted, children from families living with HIV are most likely to live in multiple risk environments. Given the interrelationship between these risk factors, a study design encompassing the conjoint and interactive effects among these risks will be considerably robust. Recent efforts at modeling data on health outcomes among HIV-positive children clearly illustrate the need to look at interactions among risk factors. For instance, a study by Cluver, Boyes, Orkin, and Sherr (2013) aimed at identifying children at the highest risk of negative health effects in the context of HIV noted that when family AIDS and poverty coexisted, children were placed at the highest risk of poor outcomes. Such studies on the interaction or additive effects of risk factors go a long way in elucidating the mechanisms through which a biomedical risk factor contributes to compromised childhood outcomes. However, the majority of recent modeling data has been based on studies of orphans. Consequently, the interaction between biomedical and psychosocial risk factors has hardly been studied. Complex modeling and longitudinal analyses to examine the association between biomedical and psychosocial risk factors would yield useful insights.

Path analytic approaches using structural equation modeling where mediated and moderated effects can be examined provide state-of-the-art ways of interpreting the contribution of biomedical and psychosocial risk factors in shaping outcomes. Mediational models attempt to clarify the relationship between an independent (variable A) and a dependent variable (variable B) through a third variable. An alternative conceptualization postulates moderator effects. Moderation analysis examines if the relationship between an independent and a dependent variable changes when conditions vary. For instance, in HIV-related studies, one may want to investigate how the presence of a caregiver who is supportive, uses adequate parenting strategies, and does not experience stigma improves neurodevelopmental outcomes for children compared to conditions where psychosocial environments are compromised. Does the psychosocial factor of caregiving quality merely serve to attenuate or intensify the neurodevelopmental outcomes of infection (moderation), or does it actually feature as a step in the causal chain between biological factors and neurodevelopmental outcomes (mediation)?

Multilevel Model. Deducing from the reviewed literature it is clear that the impact of HIV varies at different ecological levels. Complex modeling has to take into consideration the numerous ecological levels in which a child operates and how they can influence development. Guided by the theoretical underpinnings of bioecological (Bronfenbrenner, 1979) and transactional (Sameroff, 2009) models of human development, it can be hypothesized that the (neurodevelopmental, educational, and mental health) outcomes of HIV-infected and HIV-affected children will result from the interaction between individual characteristics and factors at play within the family, school, health centers, neighborhood, and even the country (since country-level policies may influence access to care services and the degree of overt stigma). For instance, how well an HIV-infected child performs in school may be partially determined by individual characteristics (e.g., coping styles, personality, and social skills), disease factors (level of disease progression and neurological involvement), household characteristics (familial SES and parental investment in the child's education), and school characteristics (stigma experience, levels of support, and inclusion vs. exclusion). Large-scale studies using multilevel approaches to evaluate data are urgently needed as insights on the influence of context on child development may provide information on useful points of intervention.

Refining Methodology. In addition to generating more data, research on the pediatric HIV population in Africa needs to build on past experience by adopting new, more precise methods, including appropriately standardized instruments and longitudinal inquiries.

Using the Right Tools to Evaluate Risk and Outcomes. One of the most significant problems in quantifying the real burden of disease in Africa is a lack of adequately standardized tools (Holding et al., 2003; Kammerer, Isquith, & Lundy, 2013; Orkin, Boyes, Cluver, & Zhang, 2014; see Chapter 5 by Matafwali & Serpell for further discussion of this topic). In addition to traditional paper and pencil approaches, neurological functioning can be assessed with neurophysiological measures such as magnetic resonance imaging, event-related potentials (ERPs), electroencephalography, and eye-tracking techniques. In Kilifi, Kenya, there has been work showing the efficacy of using ERPs in the study of the cognitive impact of infectious diseases, for example, in the study of the impact of malaria and meningitis (Kihara, de Haan, Garrashi, Neville, & Newton, 2008; Kihara et al., 2012). The expansion of technology that allows for relatively low cost, mobile data collection makes it feasible to use these methods to describe neurocognitive outcomes and biomarkers in resource-constrained environments (Bosl, 2012). Moving toward these new technologies allows the study of a greater range of outcomes and helps elucidate the structural correlates of behavioral manifestations.

Longitudinal Approaches. A significant proportion of the evidence on the impact of HIV on child development is derived from cross-sectional studies and a small number of short-term longitudinal studies. For this reason, we know little of developmental trajectories and causal pathways among this population. Many questions on the effects of HIV or exposure remain unanswered. For instance, we do not know to what extent cognitive delays impact educational outcomes. How do cognitive impairments impact health-seeking behavior, risk-taking behavior, and other important life skills? To gain a good understanding of these issues there is a need for longitudinal studies. The description of developmental trajectories across a long period of time allows for a better description of causal pathways. Additionally, the effects of HIV and its manifestations may change as children grow older. Therefore, there is a need for a lifespan approach. For instance, the major concerns for children may relate to schooling and peer relationships during middle childhood. In adolescence, the concerns relate to risk-taking sexual behavior, dating, reproductive health choices, and taking responsibility for managing their health conditions.

Concluding Remarks

This chapter attempts to highlight the need to further refine the methodological and conceptual models to be used in examining the impact of HIV on child development. The use of sophisticated conceptual and methodological models has a two-fold benefit. First, within the unique constellation of risks and resources in the local context, Africa can benefit from the existing wealth of knowledge, tools, and scales to develop her own tools to address urgent developmental needs and identify the most meaningful points of intervention. Second, studies from Africa can provide a unique perspective on risk factors and sources of resilience, given the multitude of cultural groups, rapid urbanization coexisting with rural traditional settings, rapid economic change, and demographic transitions. Such a context allows the testing of bioecological models of development to confirm their basic assumptions and make appropriate modifications and additions. Through this, we can answer the immediate needs of the larger African population, as well provide an opportunity for Africa both to learn and to expand the knowledge base on risk factors. I focused on the pediatric HIV to draw a model which allows child development psychologists to examine the complex associations among various risk factors. However, it is hoped that the lessons learned from the field of HIV can be transferred to other fields of study where biomedical risk interacts with psychosocial risk.

References

Abubakar, A. (2013). Psychosocial aspects of malnutrition among African children: Antecedents, consequences, and interventions. In M. J. Boivin & B. Giordani (Eds.), *Neuropsychology of children in Africa* (pp. 181–202). New York, NY: Springer.

Abubakar, A., Holding, P., Newton, C., Van Baar, A., & Van de Vijver, F. (2009). The role of weight for age and disease stage in poor psychomotor outcome of HIV-infected children in Kilifi, Kenya. *Developmental Medicine and Child Neurology, 51*, 968–973. doi:10.1111/j.1469-8749.2009.03333.x

Abubakar, A., Van Baar, A., Van de Vijver, F. J., Holding, P., & Newton, C. R. (2008). Paediatric HIV and neurodevelopment in sub-Saharan Africa: A systematic review. *Tropical Medicine and International Health, 13*, 880–887.

Aldenkamp, A. P., & Bodde, N. (2005). Behaviour, cognition and epilepsy. *Acta Neurologica Scandinavica, 112*, 19–25.

Allen, A. B., Finestone, M., Eloff, I., Sipsma, H., Makin, J., Triplett, K., ... Forsyth, B. W. (2014). The role of parenting in affecting the behavior and adaptive functioning of young children of HIV-infected mothers in South Africa. *AIDS and Behaviour, 18*, 605–616. doi:10.1007/s10461-013-0544-7

Bagenda, D., Nassali, A., Kalyesubula, I., Sherman, B., Drotar, D., Boivin, M. J., & Olness, K. (2006). Health, neurologic, and cognitive status of HIV-infected, long-surviving, and antiretroviral-naive Ugandan children. *Pediatrics, 117,* 729–740.

Baillieu, N., & Potterton, J. (2008). The extent of delay of language, motor, and cognitive development in HIV-positive infants. *Journal of Neurologic Physical Therapy, 32,* 118–121.

Boivin, M. J., Davies, A. G., Mokili, J. K. L., Greeen, S. D. R., Giordani, B., & Cutting, W. A. M. (1995). A preliminary evaluation of the cognitive and motor effects of pediatric HIV infection in Zairian children. *Health Psychology, 14*(1), 13–21.

Boivin, M. J., Ruel, T. D., Boal, H. E., Bangirana, P., Cao, H., Eller, L. A., ... Wong, J. K. (2010). HIV-subtype A is associated with poorer neuropsychological performance compared with subtype D in antiretroviral therapy-naive Ugandan children. *AIDS, 24,* 1163–1170.

Bosl, W. J. (2012). Neurotechnology and psychiatric biomarkers. In D. N. Ghista (Ed.), *Biomedical science, engineering and technology.* Rijeka, Croatia: InTech. doi:10.5772/19457. Retrieved from http://www.intechopen.com/books/biomedical-science-engineering-and-technology/neurotechnology-and-psychiatric-biomarkers

Boyede, G. O., Lesi, F. E., Ezeaka, C. V., & Umeh, C. S. (2013a). The neurocognitive assessment of HIV-infected school-aged Nigerian children. *World, 3,* 124–130.

Boyede, G. O., Lesi, F. E., Ezeaka, V. C., & Umeh, C. S. (2013b). Impact of sociodemographic factors on cognitive function in school-aged HIV-infected Nigerian children. *HIV/AIDS (Auckland, NZ), 5,* 145–152.

Boyede, G. O., Lesi, F. E., Ezeaka, V. C., & Umeh, C. S. (2013c). The influence of clinical staging and use of antiretroviral therapy on cognitive functioning of school-aged Nigerian children with HIV infection. *Journal of AIDS & Clinical Research, 4*(195), 2.

Boyes, M. E., & Cluver, L. D. (2013). Relationships among HIV/AIDS orphanhood, stigma, and symptoms of anxiety and depression in South African youth a longitudinal investigation using a path analysis framework. *Clinical Psychological Science, 1,* 323–330.

Bronfenbrenner, U. (1979). *The ecology of human development: Experiments by nature and design.* Cambridge, MA: Harvard University Press.

Busman, R. A., Page, C., Oka, E., Giordani, B., & Boivin, M. J. (2013). Factors contributing to the psychosocial adjustment of Ugandan preschool children with HIV/AIDS. In M. J. Boivin & B. Giordani (Eds.), *Neuropsychology of children in Africa* (pp. 95–115). New York, NY: Springer.

Cluver, L., Boyes, M., Orkin, M., & Sherr, L. (2013). Poverty, AIDS and child health: Identifying highest-risk children in South Africa. *South African Medical Journal, 103,* 910–915. doi:10.7196/samj.7045

Cluver, L., & Gardner, F. (2006). The psychological well-being of children orphaned by AIDS in Cape Town, South Africa. *Annals of General Psychiatry, 5,* 8. doi:10.1186/1744-/859X-5-8

Cluver, L., Gardner, F., & Operario, D. (2007). Psychological distress amongst AIDS-orphaned children in urban South Africa. *Journal of Child Psychology and Psychiatry, 48,* 755–763. doi:10.1111/j.1469-7610.2007.01757.x

Cluver, L., Orkin, M., Boyes, M. E., Sherr, L., Makasi, D., & Nikelo, J. (2013). Pathways from parental AIDS to child psychological, educational and sexual risk: Developing an empirically-based interactive theoretical model. *Social Science & Medicine, 87,* 185–193. doi:10.1016/j.socscimed.2013.03.028

Cluver, L. D., Orkin, M., Gardner, F., & Boyes, M. E. (2012). Persisting mental health problems among AIDS-orphaned children in South Africa. *Journal of Child Psychology and Psychiatry, 53,* 363–370. doi:10.1111/j.1469-7610.2011.02459.x

Devendra, A., Makawa, A., Kazembe, P. N., Calles, N. R., & Kuper, H. (2013). HIV and childhood disability: A case-controlled study at a paediatric antiretroviral therapy centre in Lilongwe, Malawi. *PLoS One, 8*(12), e84024.

Drotar, D., Olness, K., Wiznitzer, M., Guay, L., Marum, L., Svilar, G., ... Kiziri-Mayengo, R. (1997). Neurodevelopmental outcomes of Ugandan infants with human immunodeficiency virus type 1 infection. *Pediatrics, 100*, E5.

Drotar, D., Olness, K., Wiznitzer, M., Schatschneider, C., Marum, L., Guay, L., ... Mayengo, R. K. (1999). Neurodevelopmental outcomes of Ugandan infants with HIV infection: An application of growth curve analysis. *Health Psychology, 18*, 114–121.

Ferguson, G., & Jelsma, J. (2009). The prevalence of motor delay among HIV infected children living in Cape Town, South Africa. *International Journal of Rehabilitation Research, 32*, 108–114.

Filteau, S. (2009). The HIV-exposed, uninfected African child. *Tropical Medicine & International Health, 14*, 276–287.

Goodman, R. (1997). The Strengths and Difficulties Questionnaire: A research note. *Journal of Child Psychology and Psychiatry, 38*, 581–586.

Guo, Y., Li, X., & Sherr, L. (2012). The impact of HIV/AIDS on children's educational outcome: A critical review of global literature. *AIDS Care, 24*, 993–1012. doi:10.1080/09540121.2012.668170

Hardy, D. J., & Vance, D. E. (2009). The neuropsychology of HIV/AIDS in older adults. *Neuropsychological Review, 19*, 263–272. doi:10.1007/s11065-009-9087-0

Herrmann, S., McKinnon, E., Hyland, N. B., Lalanne, C., Mallal, S., Nolan, D., ... Duracinsky, M. (2013). HIV-related stigma and physical symptoms have a persistent influence on health-related quality of life in Australians with HIV infection. *Health and Quality of Outcomes, 11*, 1–13.

Hoare, J., Fouche, J.-P., Spottiswoode, B., Donald, K., Philipps, N., Bezuidenhout, H., ... Schrieff, L. (2012). A diffusion tensor imaging and neurocognitive study of HIV-positive children who are HAART-naïve "slow progressors." *Journal of Neurovirology, 18*, 205–212.

Holding, P. A., Taylor, H. G., Kazungu, S. D., Mkala, T., Gona, J., Mwamunye, B., ... Stevenson, J. (2003). Assessing cognitive outcomes in a rural African population: Development of a neuropsychological battery in Kilifi District. *Journal of International Neuropsychological Society, 10*, 246–260.

Holzemer, W. L., Makoae, L. N., Greeff, M., Dlamini, P. S., Kohi, T. W., Chirwa, M. L., ... Uys, L. R. (2009). Measuring HIV stigma for PLHAs and nurses over time in five African countries. *SAHARA: Journal of Social Aspects of HIV/AIDS Research Alliance, 6*, 76–82.

Jelsma, J., Davids, N., & Ferguson, G. (2011). The motor development of orphaned children with and without HIV: Pilot exploration of foster care and residential placement. *BMC Pediatrics, 11*, 11.

Kabue, M. M., Buck, W. C., Wanless, S. R., Cox, C. M., McCollum, E. D., Caviness, A. C., ... Devlin, A. (2012). Mortality and clinical outcomes in HIV-infected children on antiretroviral therapy in Malawi, Lesotho, and Swaziland. *Pediatrics, 130*, e591–e599.

Kamau, J. W., Kuria, W., Mathai, M., Atwoli, L., & Kangethe, R. (2012). Psychiatric morbidity among HIV-infected children and adolescents in a resource-poor Kenyan urban community. *AIDS Care, 24*, 836–842.

Kammerer, B., Isquith, P. K., & Lundy, S. (2013). Approaches to assessment of very young children in Africa in the context of HIV. In M. J. Boivin & B. Giordani (Eds.), *Neuropsychology of children in Africa* (pp. 17–36). New York, NY: Springer.

Kandawasvika, G. Q., Kuona, P., Chandiwana, P., Masanganise, M., Gumbo, F. Z., Mapingure, M. P., ... Stray-Pedersen, B. (2014). The burden and predictors of cognitive impairment among 6- to 8-year-old children infected and uninfected with HIV from Harare, Zimbabwe: A cross-sectional study. *Child Neuropsychology*. doi:10.1080/09297049.2013.876493

Kandawasvika, G. Q., Ogundipe, E., Gumbo, F. Z., Kurewa, E. N., Mapingure, M. P., & Stray-Pedersen, B. (2011). Neurodevelopmental impairment among infants born to mothers infected with human immunodeficiency virus and uninfected mothers from three peri-urban primary care clinics in Harare, Zimbabwe. *Developmental Medicine & Child Neurology, 53,* 1046–1052.

Kihara, M., Carter, J., & Newton, C. (2006). The effects of *Plasmodium Falciparium* on cognition: A systematic review. *Tropical Medicine & International Health, 11,* 386–397.

Kihara, M., de Haan, M., Garrashi, H. H., Neville, B. G., & Newton, C. R. (2008). Cognitive deficits following exposure to malaria with neurological involvement: An event related potentials study. *BMC Proceedings, 2*(Suppl. 1), P30.

Kihara, M., de Haan, M., Were, E. O., Garrashi, H. H., Neville, B. G., & Newton, C. R. (2012). Cognitive deficits following exposure to pneumococcal meningitis: An event-related potential study. *BMC Infectious Diseases, 12*(1), 79.

Laughton, B., Cornell, M., Grove, D., Kidd, M., Springer, P. E., Dobbels, E., ... Cotton, M. F. (2012). Early antiretroviral therapy improves neurodevelopmental outcomes in infants. *AIDS, 26,* 1685–1690.

Le Doaré, K., Bland, R., & Newell, M.-L. (2012). Neurodevelopment in children born to HIV-infected mothers by infection and treatment status. *Pediatrics, 130,* e1326–e1344.

Li, X., Huang, L., Wang, H., Fennie, K. P., He, G., & Williams, A. B. (2011). Stigma mediates the relationship between self-efficacy, medication adherence, and quality of life among people living with HIV/AIDS in China. *AIDS Patient Care and STDs, 25,* 665–671.

Lowick, S., Sawry, S., & Meyers, T. (2012). Neurodevelopmental delay among HIV-infected preschool children receiving antiretroviral therapy and healthy preschool children in Soweto, South Africa. *Psychology, Health & Medicine, 17,* 599–610.

McGrath, N., Fawzi, W. W., Bellinger, D., Robins, J., Msamanga, G. I., Manji, K., & Tronick, E. (2006). The timing of mother-to-child transmission of human immunodeficiency virus infection and the neurodevelopment of children in Tanzania. *The Pediatric Iinfectious Disease Journal, 25,* 47–52.

Menon, A., Glazebrook, C., Campain, N., & Ngoma, M. (2007). Mental health and disclosure of HIV status in Zambian adolescents with HIV infection: Implications for peer-support programs. *Journal of Acquired Immune Deficiency Syndromes, 46,* 349–354. doi:10.1097/QAI.0b013e3181565df0

Menon, A., Glazebrook, C., & Ngoma, M. S. (2009). Mental health of HIV positive adolescents in Zambia. *Medical Journal of Zambia, 36,* 151–156.

Msellati, P., Lepage, P., Deo-Gratias, H., Van Goethem, C., Van de Perre, P., & Dabis, F. (1993). Neurodevelopmental testing of children born to human immunodeficiency virus Type 1 seropositive and seronegative mothers: A prospective cohort study in Kigali, Rwanda. *Pediatrics, 92,* 843–848.

Musisi, S., & Kinyanda, E. (2009). Emotional and behavioral disorders in HIV seropositive adolescents in urban Uganda. *East African Medical Journal, 86,* 16–24.

Mwaniki, M. K., Atieno, M., Lawn, J. E., & Newton, C. R. (2012). Long-term neurodevelopmental outcomes after intrauterine and neonatal insults: A systematic review. *The Lancet, 379,* 445–452.

Orkin, M., Boyes, M. E., Cluver, L. D., & Zhang, Y. (2014). Pathways to poor educational outcomes for HIV/AIDS-affected youth in South Africa. *AIDS Care, 26,* 343–350. doi:10.1080/09540121.2013.824533

Potterton, J., Stewart, A., Cooper, P., Goldberg, L., Gajdosik, C., & Baillieu, N. (2009). Neurodevelopmental delay in children infected with human immunodeficiency virus in Soweto, South Africa. *Vulnerable Children and Youth Studies, 4,* 48–57.

Puffer, E. S., Drabkin, A. S., Stashko, A. L., Broverman, S. A., Ogwang-Odhiambo, R. A., & Sikkema, K. J. (2012). Orphan status, HIV risk behavior, and mental health among adolescents in rural Kenya. *Journal of Pediatric Psychology, 37,* 868–878.

Ruel, T. D., Boivin, M. J., Boal, H. E., Bangirana, P., Charlebois, E., Havlir, D. V., ... Wong, J. K. (2012). Neurocognitive and motor deficits in HIV-infected Ugandan children with high CD4 cell counts. *Clinical Infectious Diseases: An Official Publication of the Infectious Diseases Society of America, 54,* 1001–1009. doi:10.1093/cid/cir1037

Sameroff, A. E. (2009). *The transactional model of development: How children and contexts shape each other.* Washington, DC: American Psychological Association.

Seth, P., Kidder, D., Pals, S., Parent, J., Mbatia, R., Chesang, K., . . . Bachanas, P. (2014). Psychosocial functioning and depressive symptoms among HIV-positive persons receiving care and treatment in Kenya, Namibia, and Tanzania. *Prevention Science, 15,* 318–328. doi:10.1007/s11121-013-0420-8

Sherr, L., Croome, N., Parra-Castaneda, K., Bradshaw, K., & Herrero-Romero, R. (2014). Developmental challenges in HIV infected children—An updated systematic review. *Children and Youth Services Review, 45,* 74–89.

Smith, L., Adnams, C., & Eley, B. (2008). Neurological and neurocognitive function of HIV-infected children commenced on antiretroviral therapy. *South African Journal of Child Health, 2,* 108–113.

Stein, A., Krebs, G., Richter, L., Tomkins, A., Rochat, T., & Bennish, M. L. (2005). Babies of a pandemic. *Archives of Disease in Childhood, 90,* 116–118.

Sullivan, E. V. (2009). Special section of Neuropsychology Review on HIV/NeuroAIDS. *Neuropsychology Review, 19,* 143–249. doi:10.1007/s11065-009-9104-3

UNAIDS. (2012). *Report on the global AIDS epidemic.* Retrieved from www.unaids.org/en/resources/publications/2012/name,76121,en.asp

Van Rie, A., Dow, A., Mupuala, A., & Stewart, P. (2009). Neurodevelopmental trajectory of HIV-infected children accessing care in Kinshasa, Democratic Republic of Congo. *Journal of Acquired Immune Deficiency Syndromes, 52*(5), 636–642.

Van Rie, A., Mupuala, A., & Dow, A. (2008). Impact of the HIV/AIDS epidemic on the neurodevelopment of preschool-aged children in Kinshasa, Democratic Republic of the Congo. *Pediatrics, 122,* e123–e128.

Walker, S. P., Wachs, T. D., Meeks Gardner, J., Lozoff, B., Wasserman, G. A., Pollitt, E., & Carter, J. A. (2007). Child development: Risk factors for adverse outcomes in developing countries. *The Lancet, 369,* 145–157.

Whitehead, N., Potterton, J., & Coovadia, A. (2014). The neurodevelopment of HIV-infected infants on HAART compared to HIV-exposed but uninfected infants. *AIDS Care, 26,* 497–504.

Woods, S. P., Moore, D. J., Weber, E., & Grant, I. (2009). Cognitive neuropsychology of HIV-associated neurocognitive disorders. *Neuropsychological Review, 19,* 152–168. doi:10.1007/s11065-009-9102-5

AMINA ABUBAKAR is a postdoctoral research fellow at the Centre for Geographic Medicine Research-Coast, KEMRI/Wellcome Trust Research Progamme, Kilifi, Kenya.

Ng'asike, J. T. (2014). African early childhood development curriculum and pedagogy for Turkana nomadic pastoralist communities of Kenya. In R. Serpell & K. Marfo (Eds.), *Child development in Africa: Views from inside. New Directions for Child and Adolescent Development*, 146, 43–60.

3

African Early Childhood Development Curriculum and Pedagogy for Turkana Nomadic Pastoralist Communities of Kenya

John T. Ng'asike

Abstract

Western conceptions of child development and the models of early education they engender predominantly shape services for young children in the first eight years of life all over Africa. This chapter brings a reconceptualist perspective to the critique of Kenya's continuing failure to ground early childhood programs and services in local cultural conceptions, developmental values, childrearing practices, and the practical day-to-day realities of children's learning through participation and apprenticeship in the contexts of family routines, community experiences, and economic survival activities. The chapter draws on work I have conducted in nomadic pastoralist communities in Kenya. That research reveals the disconcerting reality that (a) early childhood education programs privilege Western pedagogical practices over equally effective and locally more relevant ones, and (b) local communities are increasingly resentful of an educational system that alienates their children from their cultural roots in the name of modernization. Asserting the educational value of indigenous knowledge, I present a framework for integrating that knowledge and the naturalistic learning processes in local contexts into instructional programs in formal ECE settings. © 2014 Wiley Periodicals, Inc.

This chapter presents a critique of Western curriculum models for early childhood education (ECE) and offers a proposal for an alternative approach to ECE curriculum in pastoralist communities. I use examples from my native Turkana pastoralist indigenous knowledge, beliefs, and cultural practices to argue for a contextually and culturally relevant early childhood curriculum and pedagogy. Although Africa has responded strongly to international conventions and treaties to commit herself to ECE, the challenge is the relevance of the curricular content and pedagogical approaches adopted in various African countries. For example, I am concerned that the philosophy and vision of early childhood curriculum in Africa overly reflect Western ways of socializing and educating children. The reasoning in this chapter is grounded in theoretical arguments of a socio-, eco-, or ethnocultural nature (e.g., Harkness & Super, 2002; Rogoff, 2003; Vygotsky, 1978; Weisner, 2002), supporting culture as the basis for development. Using *"funds of knowledge"* (González, Moll, & Amanti, 2005) as a social capital construct for theorizing about resources within households, I make a case for affirming Turkana children's culture as the foundation for their education. Focusing on cultural survival activities around livestock and the Turkana calendar, I demonstrate the possibility of a contextually relevant curriculum for Turkana pastoralist nomadic children. A comparison between the official ECE curriculum content in Kenya and Turkana cultural knowledge, beliefs, and practices reveals major similarities, on which I draw to establish a justification for the use of Turkana culture in science curriculum content within Kenya's formal ECE system.

Overview of Western Models of Early Childhood Education in Africa

Driven by the need to make commitments to international agreements on children, as mandated by the United Nations Convention on the Rights of Children (UNCRC), the African Charter, and the Millennium Development Goals (MDGs), many African countries are expanding and improving early childhood care and education especially to reach vulnerable and marginalized children. At the center of this trend is the desire to ensure equity in education provision by increasing schooling success and reducing dropout rates and grade repetition across diverse socioeconomic backgrounds (Jaramillo & Mingat, 2008; MacNaughton, Hughes, & Smith, 2007).

At various world fora, including Education for All and the Dakar conference, and with support from the World Bank, UNICEF, UNESCO, ADEA, and WGECD (Working Group on Early Childhood Development), African countries have made commitments to develop and implement early childhood development (ECD) policies (Garcia, Pence, & Evans, 2008; Pence et al., 2004). However, even though ECD policies in Africa focus on curriculum based on play and integrated holistic approaches, the mode of implementation varies in terms of the governmental ministry with primary responsibility for ECD policies and programs (Garcia et al., 2008). In addition, the level of investment also varies as many countries continue to give ECD a lower priority in comparison to primary and secondary education. For example, Kenya, South Africa, Zimbabwe, and Lesotho have ECD policy anchored in the Ministry of Education. The focus of ECD in these countries is on education rather than holistic development. But Ghana, Namibia, Mauritius, and a few others which appear to demonstrate strong ECD programs have their policies in ministries other than the Ministry of Education. For example, in Ghana, the Ministry of Women and Children's Affairs is responsible for ECD, the Ministry of Gender Equality and Child Welfare is implementing ECD in Namibia, and the Ministry of Women's Rights, Child Development and Family Welfare is responsible for ECD in Mauritius (Garcia et al., 2008). The ECD approach in these three latter countries has been to address children's programs within a family and child rights framework.

Nearly all African countries face various challenges, including the following: establishing a coordinating body for ECD, implementing a holistic integrated ECD approach, making decisions about the appropriate responsible ministry, ensuring that ECD is free, and ensuring curriculum quality and teacher training. Furthermore, although countries appear to respond to international demands to implement the educational rights of children through a robust ECE curriculum, a major criticism is that programs are based too closely on Western ideologies, with policies driven and funded by the World Bank and related multinational agencies, disregarding the uniqueness of each individual country's contexts (Biersteker, Ngaruiya, Sebatane, & Gudyanga, 2008; Garcia et al., 2008; Pence et al., 2004; Swadener, Wachira, Kabiru, & Njenga, 2008). The emphasis placed on the use of play in learning in ECE interventions in Africa has been questioned as reflecting a model directed by a Euro-American popular cultural narrative of "developmentally appropriate" practices (Samuelsson & Carlsson, 2008). As a result, a Western style of schooling continues to be the foundation of African children's education, while African cultures including local indigenous knowledge are largely disregarded (Dyer, 2006; Krätli, 2000, 2001; Marfo & Biersteker, 2011; Nsamenang, 2008, 2011a, 2011b). Indeed, the philosophy and vision of ECE do not appear to come from within Africa. Instead, the goal appears to be to place the socialization of African children in the hands of educational institutions, religious organizations, and the media informed by a Western ideology of modernization. The consequence is the extermination of African ways of bringing up children in schools for African children, a situation leading to alienation of parents from their school-age children.

Evidence from ethnographic studies conducted in Turkana (e.g., Dyer, 2006; Marianna, 2010; Ng'asike, 2010) suggests that a school-based education system framed on Western ideologies has alienated Turkana children from their families. Educated individuals in Turkana are not necessarily successful as proclaimed by popular narratives of governments, missionaries, and child rights agencies that present education as the panacea for success in Africa. According to Marianna (2010), the Turkana are worried that *Akuj* (God) is annoyed because of the increasing abuse of alcohol, increased rate of crime, unemployment, and the emergence of informal marriages that characterize the life of schooled youth and school dropouts in Turkana. The perception of the local community is that schools, the emergence of modernity, Christianity, and urbanization have made the youth corrupted, "overheated," and alcoholic, in addition to the loss of respect for the cultural norms and customs. The resulting idleness and unemployment are leading to increased crime. The behavior of the youth has attracted the wrath of *Akuj* to punish the community through frequent drought and hunger in Turkana communities. As a result, the community has become dependent on food handouts by the government and relief agencies. Poverty has contributed to the vulnerability of the community which can no longer be in charge of its development affairs and instead has turned to depend on Christianization, modernization, urbanization, and foreign interventions.

Although Turkana pastoralists acknowledge that education can lead to jobs that will translate to money which they can use to purchase livestock to stabilize their herds after the animals have been depleted by drought, Turkana families continue to experience negative effects of education as manifested by the behavior of many of their children who complete the formal school system. After families have made sacrifices to send their children to school, many children do not manage to find a job after school. As a result, boys are not able to gather a proper bride price for the mothers of their children and thus lose any right to their offspring. According to Marianna (2010), girls on the other hand find poor boyfriends who cannot marry or take care of them, necessitating the intervention of their families to offer material support to stabilize their marriages. Besides, the schooled youth have proved to be unproductive in the everyday pastoralists' economy and are unable to contribute to the survival of their families compared to uneducated youth. The experience of the Turkana families and their youth calls for a rethinking of the goals of education in Africa, especially in communities that continue to be slow in embracing modernization.

However, Western education continues to thrive in Kenya, despite the challenges facing Turkana families, as the educated elite find the Turkana argument archaic and retrogressive. As a result, ECE is rapidly developing into formal educational institutions, where children aged 0–6 years are prepared for school readiness in preprimary classes across the country. The ECD curriculum model in Kenya is articulated in a policy framework (Republic of Kenya, 2005) that envisages a cross-sector coordination of various institutions offering services for young children through an integrated service delivery strategy that encompasses child protection, nutrition, health, and education. But in Kenya, the reality is that the holistic approach remains a theoretical argument as young children are receiving care outside the family in preprimary classes using approaches that are largely Western and didactic in nature. The care of children outside the family has been accelerated by working women especially in urban areas and escalating poverty levels in Kenyan rural families. Although ECD provision in Kenya is not yet compulsory (Biersteker et al., 2008), increasing numbers of public and private primary schools are conducting admission interviews with children seeking to join Standard One classes as a result of the growing academic competition in ECD (Pence et al., 2004). Concerns are being raised regarding the whereabouts of those children who fail in these interviews. My interviews with teachers revealed that they could not account for where these children disappear to after they are turned away. Child rights continue to be elusive in Kenya as children are denied education as early as at the ECD levels. The practice by primary school teachers and private school authorities of conducting such selective interviews with the full knowledge of the Ministry of Education officials and without government intervention appears to be a glaring injustice. As a result, educationally disadvantaged pastoralist communities like the Turkana find it hard to engage with a system of education that is impossible to comprehend.

Context and Curriculum Activities in Rural ECD Centers in Nomadic Pastoralist Communities. Academic demands of the education system in Kenya create challenges in ECE curriculum interpretation across the country. Even though the Kenya Institute of Curriculum Development expects teachers to contextualize learning to reflect the cultural needs and local experiences of children (Ministry of Education & UNICEF, 2008), curriculum and instruction in most of the ECD centers in rural areas of Kenya remain didactic and academic. For example, in a typical ECD center in Kenya, irrespective of context, children receive direct instruction in the English language. Textbooks are written in English and stories read to children are of Western content. To enhance performance at the interviews, children in rural ECD centers recite the letters of the alphabet and number symbols written on the chalkboard from morning (8 o'clock) to lunch break (12 o'clock). In some of the preprimary classes I visited in Turkana, the alphabets and numerals (1 to 100) have been written with a permanent marker on the chalkboard for children to recite daily.

The classrooms are usually empty halls without furniture or mats for children to sit on. There is no display of learning materials, as the classroom walls of preprimary classes in Turkana are overventilated with open spaces without window shutters. During a windy or rainy day, for example, learning is nearly impossible as wind and rain flow into the classrooms and wind pulls down any resources hung on the overventilated walls. The consequences of poor instructional approaches and unfriendly classroom conditions are that young children experience learning apathy as they crowd in congested classrooms (Ng'asike, 2010). Lack of teachers compounds the challenges of learning as the pastoralist children simply hang around

Standard One classes to wait for meals and after they have had their lunch they immediately move to the dry river courses to engage in what they like best, which is natural play with sand and water at the riverbed.

In this natural play context, young nomadic children hunt birds and squirrels, collect insects, and engage in livestock herding. Observed streaming to the river courses, it is as if schools lock children in prison and time out of school is time to catch up with natural learning that is interesting, creative, and meaningful. Learning arrangements at the ECD centers are in sharp contrast with the everyday activities of children's life out of school. In ECD centers, for example, children's play is limited, as demands for rote memorization of alphabets and numerals take the center stage of their learning despite the availability of folklore materials from local cultures. For instance, the indigenous traditional knowledge with a rich base of folktales, songs, dances, myths, beliefs, knowledge of nature, environment, the universe, soil, water, plants, and others is not mentioned in any form in the education of African children. This cultural knowledge is invisible in African educational institutions as if it did not exist. The irony is that ECD children continue to learn at the doorstep of their own cultures in English from curriculum content based on Western ideology to the extent that the knowledge of families in the villages is ignored by the oppressive education system.

For example, I observed and interviewed a local middle-aged mother who, although only semiliterate, had been hired by the primary school to teach a preprimary class. During a class session I observed, the woman read a story to children about a man climbing a mango tree. Later, when I asked her whether she had seen a mango tree and a mango fruit, the woman had no idea of what this tree and its fruits look like. I asked her why she was teaching the children a story of a plant she had never seen and what meaning she thought this story had for the children. The woman responded that this was the book she was given and the only reading material available in the school. I asked her if there are trees with fruits in the community that people climb. She replied that they are there in plenty, and she mentioned *Egol* (palm trees). She also mentioned that there are plenty of local cultural stories that she would have narrated to the children if she was given a chance.

This was a case of a local resource not well utilized. This woman was obviously one of the elders who could be instrumental in providing rich Turkana cultural knowledge important in the development of these young children. For example, the ethnographic report presented here involves trees with which Turkana children are very familiar and could also serve the additional function of educating the children about local rituals associated with childbirth and the importance of fire in childbirth:

> When a child is born, the placenta is buried in the soil, usually under the tree called **engomo**, so that mother and child are protected against the evil eye and any bad intention. If there is not **engomo** tree, any other tree would do.

After this, a traditional fire is lit up from two wooden sticks. These are the *loberu* and the *lokile*, the wife and the husband. *Loberu* lays down, and *lokile* enters in a small hole in *loberu*, and the person in charge so can make the fire. Everyone can perform this work, but the fire cannot be lent to anyone. (Marianna, 2010, p. 46)

This indigenous narrative has the potential to teach children deep understandings of their cultural history, traditions, values, trees, fire making, soil, friction, and the value of conservation of natural ecosystems. ECD centers hardly teach material like this (see Chapter 4 for further examples of relevant local knowledge excluded from African ECD curricula). The teaching is dry and thin, and focuses mainly on rote memorization of factual information. The woman at the preprimary school was aware of these narratives, but the forces of hegemony compelled her to teach Turkana children in a way that disrupts the spiritual harmony of the children's worldview.

Theoretical Support for Consideration of Turkana Cultural Knowledge and Practices

Privileging the Western concept of ECE over other cultures as advocated in the Kenyan ECD curriculum runs contrary to contemporary theory of child development in cultural context. Drawing from the work of Vygotsky (1978), researchers such as Bruner (1990), Moll and colleagues (Moll, Amanti, Neff, & Gonzalez, 2005), and Rogoff (2003) argue that individual development cannot be separated from the social, cultural, and historical contexts in which it belongs. Individuals are influenced by the kind of activities they engage with in everyday life within their cultural institutions. Vygotsky's theory underscored the role of culture in providing individuals with the cognitive toolkit for constructing understandings of their worlds and conceptions about themselves. According to Vygotsky, human intellectual development is a result of mediation of actions through artifacts and practices of the everyday cultural life of people. Cognitive skills rely on cultural inventions, such as literacy, mathematics, mnemonic skills, problem solving, creativity, and reasoning (Rogoff, 2003). Rogoff further extends Vygotsky's argument by pointing out that humans are biologically cultural and that cultural and biological characteristics are mutually dependent. Children learn to use the tools acquired through their cultural experiences to interact with adults, peers, and significant others to continue learning within the zone of proximal development (Vygotsky, 1978). Human beings use social processes and cultural resources of all kinds in helping children construct meaning of their worlds (González et al., 2005).

At the heart of Vygotsky's theory are the resources available at the household level within the everyday cultural experiences of families and children that can be harnessed to mediate children's learning. "Funds of knowledge" are defined as the "historical accumulated and culturally developed bodies of knowledge and skills essential for household or for individual functioning and wellbeing" (Moll et al., 2005, p. 72). Research building on this concept emphasizes the integration of household and community resources to create instructional materials for teaching children in schools that operate in communities perceived as poor economically. The *funds of knowledge* orientation, when used as a framework to guide instructional design and delivery, provides context and relevance to classroom curriculum content. Examples are cultural artifacts, music, art, language, religion, schools, economic activities, agriculture, child care, construction, family chores, entertainment, and others (González et al., 2005).

Weisner (2002) uses ecocultural theory to explain the importance of *cultural pathways* (everyday routines with which children engage in family and community life) for learning and survival. Ethnocultural theory emphasizes that within a particular cultural context communities provide pathways for children's optimal development. According to the concept of *parental ethnotheories* (Harkness & Super, 2002), parenting is culturally constructed, and children's socialization and development involve a process of cultural assimilation or enculturation. Weisner, Harkness, and Super, whose ethnographic research has included work in Africa, agree with Vygotsky and Rogoff on the role of culture as a socializing agent and the foundation on which families bring up their children. These theories offer a conceptual framework for interpreting the importance of the cultural practices of Turkana families in educating young children. Turkana pastoralists' lifestyles provide children the pathways for development which include everyday activities of their culture. Some of these pathways involve participation in economic activities used by Turkana families for survival (e.g., animal husbandry, agriculture, and hunting), sharing responsibility for family household chores, and engagement with natural phenomena (e.g., knowledge of weather and seasons).

Turkana Pastoralists' Children Everyday Cultural Knowledge and Learning Styles. Drawing from the literature and theoretical grounding in support of context and culture as key in human development, in this section I make a case for a curriculum and pedagogy of Turkana nomads as a model African curriculum in ECE. I draw from my ethnographic research work in Turkana (Ng'asike, 2010) and the work of Marianna (2010). The research involved studying the social-cultural activities of the Turkana nomads and how the activities inform children's education in a pastoralist community. Nomadic people live by hunting, livestock herding, and fruit gathering, among their many everyday survival activities. To survive in a pastoralist nomadic lifestyle, the skill of herding livestock is mastered by children as they grow from childhood through adulthood. Livestock herding skills progressively increase in complexity and in precision as children grow older. By being present around parents and observing adults interact with livestock, children master the physical as well as the psychological characteristics of a stock to the extent that they can tell any little scars, cracks, and cuts inflicted on the skin or at the hoof of an animal. On a daily basis, children form a repertoire of the physiological characteristics of their stock. For example, it is the scars an animal gets from injury, small or big, which form permanent marks on its body after healing and other birth features that children and adults use when studying a particular species of livestock to master the appearance and the properties the herder requires to fully identify his or her stock. After studying their livestock for a long time children as well as adults know by looking at the hoof prints on the ground that this animal belongs to their herd or it is a straying stock from a different herd. Turkana herdsmen and their children study livestock hoof prints with almost equal accuracy to the scientist studying fingerprints.

The prints made by livestock hooves on the ground can tell that this animal is from the lowland or from the highland. An elder I interviewed explained to me that animals that graze on the lowlands have long nails on their hooves and those that graze on highlands or at the foot of the slopes have smooth hooves or broken nails. The highlands are made of rough terrains of coarse sands, gravels, and boulders which eat at the hooves of the livestock to alter their shape and structure. This explains why the marks that livestock make on the ground are characterized by the sharpness or smoothness of the hooves depending on the roughness of the terrain of their grazing land. For example, a stone hitting the hoof of an animal will most likely hurt the hoof and after it heals a mark remains. This mark will be used by the herdsman to differentiate his stock from other herds. The herdsman keeps mental records of these physical changes no matter where on the animal's body the marks are located. This same skill is mastered by children as they interact with the livestock from childhood. Marks on hooves will differentiate the hooves of a herdsman's livestock from others and would assist in tracking a lost animal. Turkana herdsmen use these unique marks to trace specific livestock of their herds when they are lost or stolen. This is precisely the knowledge the children also acquire so as to become skillful in animal husbandry and help support the family.

Understanding Turkana Calendar in Early Childhood Curriculum. Teaching children knowledge of livestock, which is the core survival socioeconomic activity of the Turkana, does not happen without knowledge of the universe and the environment which is critical in livestock husbandry. The mental strategy that the nomads use to make adaptation to the harsh environmental fluctuations (Dyer, 2006) depends on the people's knowledge of the universe.

The Turkana are versed in knowledge of weather and are able to make accurate rainfall predictions which are important for both livestock and human survival (Coughenour, 2004; McCabe, 2004). Droughts or any other calamities, including epidemics, do not usually find the Turkana pastoralists unaware, as the people are able to predict future events (bad or good) reliably enough to be able to prepare the community for them. One important way of understanding the universe and weather patterns is knowledge of the calendar which the Turkana use to follow rainfall patterns and anticipate grazing patterns for their livestock. Children begin to acquire this knowledge from birth.

Table 3.1 describes the events of the Turkana calendar and presents the local names of the months and the corresponding English names. It is apparent that months of the Western calendar, to a large extent, match the Turkana months. Thus, Turkana local knowledge can be matched with Western knowledge and taught side by side, where each type of knowledge helps to strengthen the child's understanding of the world using multiple interpretations in different cultures. For example, the Turkana calendar begins in March, while the Western calendar begins in January. Each Turkana month has 28 days while the Western months vary between 28 and 31, depending on whether it is a leap year. The theory of collateral learning explains instructional approaches in which children are provided with opportunities to share knowledge of different cultures, to compare and contrast them to develop consensus of their understanding of these knowledge systems (Aikenhead, 2000; Aikenhead & Jegede, 1999; Jegede, 1997). A similar pedagogical approach has been proposed by Kawagley (2006) for Yupiaq children in Alaska. The Yupiaq people have 13 moons, while the Western calendar has 12 moons. Kawagley's curriculum has incorporated all the Yupiaq cultural knowledge (e.g., fishing and processing, weather, mental healing, native diet, and other topics) into instructional content.

Collateral learning theory argued that information should be presented to children in the manner in which they appear naturally so that children develop their own rationale regarding how they will use these different types of valid ideas for learning. Children require exposure to all kinds of cultural understanding for holistic development. Some of the knowledge will prepare them for national examinations, and other knowledge will be skills for survival at home and in the world. Aikenhead (2001) proposed the pedagogy of a culture broker in which a science teacher identifies the colonizer and the colonized and teaches the science of each culture. In this way, the culture broker acknowledges issues of social power and privilege in the science classroom. In a bicultural study of African refugee children learning in Canadian elementary and early childhood schools, Hennig and Kirova (2012) and Kirova (2010) reported that culture brokers brought African artifacts and other materials from African culture to help the refugee children learn in a context of their African culture while in a different continent away from Africa. The children learned creatively and were able to learn English when using their cultural materials without difficulty.

Pedagogical Value of Turkana Children's Indigenous Knowledge in ECD. African pedagogy proposed in science education by Jegede (1994) argued for alternative conceptions and constructivism in science instruction in which an individual's perception of knowledge is drawn from his/her sociocultural environment. According to Jegede (1994), "one way to help eradicate the fear or apprehension African children have towards science is to identify the elements of a number of fundamental scientific principles

Table 3.1. Turkana Months and Seasons

Seasons	Months English	Months Turkana	Characteristics of Turkana Months
Wet season Akiporo	March	Lomaruk	The month of hunger. The clouds are starting to form. The rains are expected. Livestock (camels) are slaughtered for food as hunger strikes.
	April	Titima	The rains start to fall. The land turns green with plenty of grazing pasture for livestock. Milk is plentiful in the community. People are happy as food is available even from plants.
	May	El-el	The flowering month. The land is beautiful. Livestock are reproducing. Environment is rich in fauna and flora.
	June	Lochoto	*Lochoto* means muddy. Women and children wade in the mud as they milk the livestock. The community continues to experience rain storms. Kids and calves keep young children very busy.
	July	Losuban	The month of *offering* sacrifices to "God." Time to thank "God" for the rains and food availability. Celebrations including weddings and spiritual ceremonies mark community traditional activities. Unpaid dowries are paid to the brides' families.
	August	Lotiak	*Lotiak* means to separate wet season from dry season. The season of plenty and happiness ends, and food becomes scarce. Blood is extracted from goats, camels, and cows to supplement the little milk available from the stock. The end to friendship, and men leave their homes to look for pastures and food.
Dry season Akamu	September	Lolong'u	*Lolong'u* means the middle of wet season and dry season. Hunger is approaching as the food is limited. Animals are no longer capable of providing milk or blood extracts.
	October	Lopo	*Lopo* means cook or boil for longer hours. It is associated with cooking hard foods like wild fruits. People resort to hunting wild animals and gathering of wild fruits. Cooking wild fruits can be a hard task. Cooking is done by the water source as plenty of water might be necessary.
	November	Lorara	*Lorara* is falling fruits, seeds, leaves, and so on. Livestock (goats and sheep) depend on dry ripe fruits of acacia trees. People dry plant seeds for livestock and for human consumption. People resort to dried foods such as milk.

(Continued)

Table 3.1. Continued

Seasons	Months		Characteristics of Turkana Months
	English	Turkana	
	December	Lomuk	Lomuk means cover. All the fruit leaves disappear, and trees start to blossom to form canopies. This is the time for adaptation of plants and livestock to survive dry weather.
	January	Lokwang	Lokwang means white to signify dryness associated with the month. There is severe hunger in the community. Children are malnourished. Livestock is slaughtered to sustain the families against the drought.
	February	Lodunge	Lodung'e is putting off the dry season. The dry season comes to an end ushering in the start of a wet season.

Source: Ng'asike (2010) and Marianna (2010).

in some of Africa's so called fetish, primitive, or crude practices, and to link these practices to some western science principles" (p. 128). To help African teachers implement Jegede's proposed pedagogy in early childhood centers in Turkana, I draw from my dissertation findings to argue for the connection between early childhood curriculum concepts and local indigenous knowledge of the Turkana people (Ng'asike, 2010).

Table 3.2 is an attempt to draw a comparison of some of the curriculum content of Turkana culture with topics in the Kenyan ECE science curriculum. Although the similarities are evident, the challenge is how to draw from children's experiences of their culture in teaching formal school content. If pedagogy is the quality of social engagement between adults and the children within the zone of proximal development (Marfo & Biersteker, 2011; Rogoff, 2003), African children will benefit when the local cultural experiences of children are used in providing context to scientific concepts in classroom instruction. This also includes use of cultural communication tools such as proverbs, myths, stories, songs, games, and other modes of interaction to ensure learning is culturally engaging and stimulating to children in early childhood classrooms. Another property of African pedagogy is that knowledge is passed indirectly to children through observation. In this approach, children are present around adults observing and internalizing passively the knowledge and skills of their culture. For example, children learn by observing the dances and rituals performed at ceremonies, which they role model in their sociodramatic play activities when practicing knowledge learned from school subjects. Elders also teach children directly with stories, myths, and proverbs of rich narratives from their culture using a generative and unwritten curriculum (Nsamenang, 2008, 2011a; Nsamenang & Tchombe, 2011). Elders create this generative curriculum as soon

Table 3.2. Comparison of Formal School Science Content and Turkana Everyday Cultural Practices

Kenyan Early Childhood Curriculum Content	Turkana Sociocultural Practices of Everyday Family Survival Activities, Knowledge, and Beliefs
• Human body	• Turkana body is thinner and faster, gets less sick, survives with little dietary intake, the legs are straight and the neck is upright, the body is generally hardened to withstand long hours of walking and hard nomadic pastoralist environment • Turkana fisherman is stronger although easily prone to disease attack; fisherman body is thicker, fatter, bowed legs, poor diet; fishermen are not considered friendly (hotter) • The town person/school pupil is weaker, prone to diseases, generally perceived by the herdsmen to be lazy, dandy-looking but straight; the diet of town people or of school children is perceived to be poor diet most often it is maize grains, beans, or maize flour with insufficient fats, and so on. Modernized people are considered softer and aggressive (hotter)
• Health education	• Reproduction pattern of livestock • Livestock treatment • Use of herbs in treating both humans and livestock • Birth ceremonies, placenta disposal beliefs, and so on • Infant care and feeding taboos and beliefs
• Plants	• Plants for agriculture (drought-resistant plants) • Animal pasture and plant classification • Fruit gathering
• Weather	• Studying weather patterns and clouds, rain making • The Turkana calendar
• Water	• Watering livestock • Water exploration • Rain making
• Animals	• Milking livestock • Naming livestock • Livestock treatment • Mastery of hoof prints • Mastery of animals' physical characteristics (colors, horns, facial appearance, branding and clan symbols) • Reproduction pattern of livestock • Livestock treatment • Herding and tracking livestock

(Continued)

Table 3.2. Continued

Kenyan Early Childhood Curriculum Content	Turkana Sociocultural Practices of Everyday Family Survival Activities, Knowledge, and Beliefs
• Soil	• Mastery of hoof print marks on different soils • Mastery of grazing lands • Lowlands, highlands • Mastery of grazing pastures • Mastery of plant habitats • Mastery of water exploration by studying rocks and sandy soils
• Food	• Preserving foodstuffs • Animal skinning and slaughtering • Making cheese • Drying milk, meat, fish • Tracking animals • Livestock treatment • Preserving foodstuffs • Fruit gathering • Turkana perceive their diet to be better than school diet
• Light	• Fire-making • Studying the sun to interpret weather and natural calamities
• Energy	• Fire making • Sharpening with stones or hard steel
• Sound	• Mastery of livestock sounds
• Air	• Strong sense of the environment and livestock
• Making work easier	• Sharpening with stones or hard steel • Rabbit snares

Source: Ng'asike (2010) and Marianna (2010).

as children begin to follow the ceremonies and everyday survival activities of their families as early as they start to crawl and walk. Young preschool children in Turkana, for example, practice herding young kids of goats and milking goats with the help of their parents. When children grow into young adolescents, they perfect the skills of animal husbandry as they graduate to herding bigger animals (goats, camels, cattle). An African curriculum is generative as it is creatively designed to refine the skills of children as they participate in everyday survival household chores. African pedagogy also relies on peer and sibling teaching in which child-to-child mentorship is a core strategy through which children learn the skills of independence, intelligence, and social responsibility (Marfo & Biersteker, 2011; Nsamenang, 2008, 2011a, 2011b; Nsamenang & Tchombe, 2011; Serpell, 2011).

In the narratives of the Turkana calendar, learning consists of intense understanding of rituals as families worship and give sacrifices to God either to thank Him or to request for rain, and so on. The songs, ceremonies, myths, and stories are used by the families and the children as they follow events of nature using the calendar. The richness of the language, the culture, and the practical activities children are involved in at home make the acquisition of knowledge and skills enduring. The irony is that African cultural knowledge and pedagogy do not feature in school content in African countries (Dyer, 2006; Krätli, 2001; Marfo & Biersteker, 2011; Nsamenang, 2008; Ntarangwi, 2004). In Kenya, the academic environment appears to take priority over authentic learning. ECD centers teach children to memorize alphabets and numerals as a routine.

Another example to learn from is a science curriculum developed by Aikenhead (2001) in Alaska, referred to as "rekindling traditions," in which Aikenhead, with support from elders, taught alongside Western knowledge Aboriginal knowledge of snowshoes, nature's hidden gifts, the night sky, survival in our land, wild rice, trapping, indigenous plants that heal, and so on. The Aborigine children used their knowledge to help discover similarities with the Western science or use the local science knowledge to critique school science knowledge. For example, Aboriginal culture has 13 moons and Western science has 12 moons. Each culture maintains the number of the moons without forcing the other to change or assimilate to the other. This is very similar to the calendar months of the Turkana children, which should be taught side by side with the Western calendar to help the child learn knowledge from a meaningful context. Rekindling curriculum is an example of a cross-cultural pedagogy that creates bridges to facilitate smooth border crossing between Western culture and indigenous cultural perspective. Humanistic, collateral, and culture brokers argue for smooth border crossing in bicultural and multicultural education (Aikenhead, 2001; Aikenhead & Jegede, 1999; Hennig & Kirova, 2012; Kirova, 2010).

Conclusion

Recent developments across the continent show that African countries have committed themselves to implementing early childhood development and education programs, even though the content of the curriculum is largely Western. In this chapter, I have presented curriculum ideas and pedagogical principles, based on the culture of Turkana nomads, as a way of integrating African culture in ECD. I have pointed out that learning environments in many rural schools in Kenya lack proper infrastructure and appropriate learning materials. The scarce resources that teachers use to teach preschool children are mainly of Western origin. English dominates the learning in early childhood as a result of the dominance of NGOs and churches in the management of ECD services in rural communities in Kenya. This chapter is intentionally provocative and aimed at challenging African educators and researchers to explore the possibility of a more African ECE system.

References

Aikenhead, G. S. (2000). Students ease in crossing cultural borders into school science. *Science Education, 85,* 180–188.

Aikenhead, G. S. (2001). Integrating Western and Aboriginal sciences: Cross-cultural science teaching. *Studies in Science Education, 26,* 1–52.

Aikenhead, G. S., & Jegede, O. J. (1999). Cross-cultural science education: A cognitive explanation of a cultural phenomenon. *Journal of Research in Science Teaching, 36,* 269–287.

Biersteker, L., Ngaruiya, S., Sebatane, E., & Gudyanga, S. (2008). Introducing preprimary classes in Africa: Opportunities and challenges. In M. Garcia, A. Pence, & J. L. Evans (Eds.), *Africa's future, Africa's challenge. Early childhood care and development in Sub-Saharan Africa* (pp. 227–248). Washington, DC: World Bank.

Bruner, J. S. (1990). *Acts of meaning.* Cambridge, MA: Harvard University Press.

Coughenour, M. (2004). The Ellis paradigm—Humans, herbivores and rangeland systems. *Journal of Range & Forage Science, 21,* 191–200.

Dyer, C. (Ed.). (2006). *The education of nomadic peoples. Current issues, future prospects.* New York, NY: Berghahn Books.

Garcia, M., Pence, A., & Evans, J. L. (Eds.). (2008). *Africa's future, Africa's challenge. Early childhood care and development in Sub-Saharan Africa.* Washington, DC: World Bank.

González, N., Moll, L. C., & Amanti, C. (Eds.). (2005). *Funds of knowledge. Theorizing practices in households, communities, and classrooms.* Mahwah, NJ: Erlbaum.

Harkness, S., & Super, C. M. (2002). Culture and parenting. In M. H. Bornstein (Ed.), *Handbook of parenting: Biology and ecology of parenting* (Vol. 2, pp. 253–280). Mahwah, NJ: Erlbaum.

Hennig, K., & Kirova, A. (2012). The role of cultural artifacts in play as tools to mediate learning in an intercultural preschool programme. *Contemporary Issues in Early Childhood, 13.* Retrieved from www.wwwords.co.uk/CIEC/content/pdfs/13/issue13_3.asp#7

Jaramillo, A., & Mingat, A. (2008). Early childhood care and education in Sub-Saharan Africa: What would it take to meet the Millennium development goals? In M. Garcia, A. Pence, & J. L. Evans (Eds.), *Africa's future, Africa's challenge. Early childhood care and development in Sub-Saharan Africa* (pp. 51–70). Washington DC: World Bank.

Jegede, O. J. (1994). African cultural perspectives and the teaching of science. In J. Solomon & G. Aikenhead (Eds.), *STS education international perspectives on reforms* (pp. 120–130). New York, NY: Teachers College Press.

Jegede, O. J. (1997). School science and the development of scientific culture: A review of contemporary science education in Africa. *International Journal of Science Education, 19*(1), 1–20.

Kawagley, A. O. (2006). *A Yupiaq worldview. A pathway to ecology and spirit* (2nd ed.). Long Gove, IL: Waveland Press.

Kirova, A. (2010). Children's representations of cultural scripts in play: Facilitating transition from home to preschool in an intercultural early learning program for refugee children. *Diaspora, Indigenous, and Minority Education, 4*(2), 1–18. Retrieved from http://dx.doi.org/10.1080/15595691003635765

Krätli, S. (2000). *Education provision to nomadic pastoralists.* Literature review (Project Contract 7528355). Washington, DC: World Bank.

Krätli, S. (2001). *Educating nomadic herders out of poverty? Culture, education, and pastoral livelihood in Turkana and Karamoja*. Institute of Development Studies, University of Sussex, UK.

MacNaughton, G., Hughes, P., & Smith, K. (2007). Early childhood professionals and children's rights: Tensions and possibilities around the United Nations General Comment No. 7 on Children's Rights. *International Journal of Early Years Education, 15*, 161–170.

Marfo, K., & Biersteker, L. (2011). Exploring culture, play, and early childhood education practice in African contexts. In S. Rogers (Ed.), *Rethinking play and pedagogy in early childhood education: Concepts, contexts and cultures* (pp. 73–86). Abingdon, UK: Routledge.

Marianna, B. (2010). *The children of Eve: Change and socialization among sedentarized Turkana children and youth* (Master's thesis). University of Bergen, Norway. Retrieved from https://bora.uib.no/handle/1956/7382

McCabe, J. M. (2004). *Cattle bring us to our enemies. Turkana ecology, politics, and raiding in a disequilibrium system*. Ann Arbor: University of Michigan Press.

Ministry of Education & UNICEF. (2008). *Forum on flexible education. Reaching nomadic populations*. Garissa, Kenya: Authors.

Moll, C. L., Amanti, C., Neff, D., & Gonzalez, N. (2005). Funds of knowledge for teaching: Using a qualitative approach to connect homes and classrooms. In N. Gonzalez, L. C. Moll, & C. Amanti (Eds.), *Funds of knowledge. Theorizing practices in households, communities, and classrooms* (pp. 71–88). Mahwah, NJ: Erlbaum.

Ng'asike, J. T. (2010). *Turkana children's sociocultural practices of pastoralist lifestyles and science curriculum and instruction in Kenyan early childhood education* (Doctoral dissertation). Arizona State University, Tucson.

Nsamenang, A. B. (2008). (Mis)Understanding ECD in Africa: The force of local and global motives. In M. Garcia, A. Pence, & J. L. Evans (Eds.), *Africa's future, Africa's challenge. Early childhood care and development in Sub-Saharan Africa* (pp. 135–149). Washington, DC: World Bank.

Nsamenang, A. B. (2011a). Developmental learning in African cultural circumstances. In A. B. Nsamenang & T. M. S. Tchombe (Eds.), *Handbook of African educational theories and practices. A generative teacher education curriculum* (pp. 233–244). Bamenda, Cameroon: Human Development Resource Centre.

Nsamenang, A. B. (2011b). Toward a philosophy for Africa's education. In A. B. Nsamenang & T. M. S. Tchombe (Eds.), *Handbook of African educational theories and practices. A generative teacher education curriculum* (pp. 55–66). Bamenda, Cameroon: Human Development Resource Centre.

Nsamenang, A. B., & Tchombe, T. M. S. (2011). Introduction: Generative pedagogy in the context of all cultures can contribute scientific knowledge of universal value. In A. B. Nsamenang & T. M. S. Tchombe (Eds.), *Handbook of African educational theories and practices. A generative teacher education curriculum* (pp. 5–21). Bamenda, Cameroon: Human Development Resource Centre.

Ntarangwi, M. (2004). The challenges of education and development in postcolonial Kenya. *Africa Development, 28*, 211–228.

Pence, A., Amponsah, M., Chalamanda, F., Habtom, A., Kameka, G., & Nankunda, H. (2004). ECD policy development and implementation in Africa. *International Journal of Educational Policy, Research, & Practice, 5*(3), 13–30.

Republic of Kenya. (2005). *Sessional Paper No. 1 of 2005 on a policy framework for education, training and research. Meeting the challenges of education, training and research in Kenya in the 21st century*. Ministry of Education, Science and Technology. Nairobi: Government Printer.

Rogoff, B. (2003). *The cultural nature of human development*. Oxford, NY: Oxford University Press.

Samuelsson, I. P., & Carlsson, M. A. (2008). The playing learning child: Towards a pedagogy of early childhood. *Scandinavian Journal of Educational Research, 52,* 623–641.
Serpell, R. (2011). Social responsibility as a dimension of intelligence, and as an educational goal: Insights from programmatic research in an African society. *Child Development Perspectives, 5,* 126–133.
Swadener, E., Wachira, P., Kabiru, M., & Njenga, A. (2008). Linking policy discourse to everyday life in Kenya: Impacts of neoliberal policies on early education and childrearing. In M. Garcia, A. Pence, & J. L. Evans (Eds.), *Africa's future, Africa's challenge. Early childhood care and development in Sub-Saharan Africa* (pp. 407–426). Washington, DC: World Bank.
Vygotsky, L. S. (1978). *Mind in society: The development of higher psychological processes.* Cambridge, MA: Harvard University Press.
Weisner, T. S. (2002). Ecocultural understanding of children's developmental pathways. *Human Development, 45,* 275–281.

JOHN T. NG'ASIKE is a lecturer in the Department of Early Childhood Studies and Primary Education, Kenyatta University, Nairobi, Kenya.

Ngwaru, J. M. (2014). Promoting children's sustainable access to early schooling in Africa: Reflections on the roles of parents in their children's early childhood care and education. In R. Serpell & K. Marfo (Eds.), *Child development in Africa: Views from inside. New Directions for Child and Adolescent Development, 146*, 61–76.

4

Promoting Children's Sustainable Access to Early Schooling in Africa: Reflections on the Roles of Parents in Their Children's Early Childhood Care and Education

Jacob Marriote Ngwaru

Abstract

Sub-Saharan Africa has predominantly rural populations unable to offer children sustainable access to early literacy and childhood care and education. Children's literacy development starts very early in life through participation and experiences in the home and preschool. My research in rural Zimbabwe, Kenya, Uganda, and Tanzania shows that the transition from home to school is compromised by acute barriers such as lack of parental participation, lack of encouragement and support from teachers, and unavailability of learning materials. However, rural homes and communities are well endowed with a stock of practices, knowledge, and skills relevant to the promotion of literacy development. In this chapter, I reflect on how to empower parents to draw on knowledge and resources within the local context to become better involved in their children's education while also empowering teachers to better recognize and take advantage of local knowledge and resources to enrich instruction and enhance meaningful learning. © 2014 Wiley Periodicals, Inc.

Education is critical to the world's attainment of the Millennium Development Goals (MDGs), more so for Sub-Saharan African countries aiming to get their economies into middle-income status by 2025. Two of the eight MDGs pertain to education—the goal of universal primary completion and the goal of gender parity in primary and secondary schooling—and are important benchmarks to align educational aspirations in Sub-Saharan Africa. Moreover, education for girls, especially, has a direct and proven impact on the goals related to child and reproductive health and environmental sustainability (UNESCO, 2010). However, the universal primary completion goal is at risk of not being achieved as long as children have no sustainable access to schooling in the first place.

The situation of poor schooling is still dire in Sub-Saharan Africa where literacy is the most neglected of the basic educational goals, as most children are unable to comprehend grade-level texts. In East Africa, for example, UWEZO Tanzania (2011) reports that only one in ten Standard Three pupils could read a basic English story, and even at Standard Seven the majority were far from achieving functional comprehension of simple prose. This has direct implications for achievement in all areas of study and by extension development (Colette, 2008). The challenges of low literacy rates are widely recognized to be greatest in Sub-Saharan Africa where both access and quality remain critical problems. The region has the highest proportion of out-of-school children, the greatest gender disparities, the highest ratio of pupils to teachers, and the lowest primary completion rates in the world (UNESCO, 2008).

The World Declaration on Education for All (UNESCO, 1990) underscored the importance of early childhood care and education (ECCE) as part of a comprehensive approach to achieving Education for All (EFA) by declaring that learning begins at birth. Early literacy development, therefore, has to be seen as one of the cornerstones of sustainable development for social transformation in low-resourced communities. This is consistent with the World Education Forum's (UNESCO, 2000) target of "expanding and improving comprehensive early childhood care and education, especially for the most vulnerable and disadvantaged children" (Goal 1, p. 15). The positive effects of ECCE programs on school readiness and performance have been documented in research studies and syntheses in the West (Karoly, Kilburn, & Cannon, 2005; Reynolds, Wang, & Walberg, 2003; Zigler, Gilliam, & Jones, 2006) but not in Sub-Saharan Africa.

Parental involvement in children's early literacy development at home and school emerged as a missing element in a set of studies in the

---

The author pays tribute to the sponsors of the two East African studies—the Hewlett Foundation through the Aga Khan Foundation for the EAQEL study; and the Department of Foreign Affairs and Trade Development, Canada (DFATD), and Aga Khan Development Network (AKDN) for the study Parent–Teacher Empowerment in Early Literacy Development in Southern Tanzania.

Southeastern subregion of Africa (Ngwaru, 2010; Ngwaru, Mweru, & Oluga, 2013; Ngwaru & Njoroge, 2011). In this chapter, I reflect on those studies to highlight the significant value of early childhood education and the crucial role that parents can play at home and school, especially if they have been empowered to embrace the pedagogies of cooperation. I argue that a new kind of relationship is required between teachers and parents to transform the traditional negative dominant relations of power to relations of collaboration in the schools.

Background to the Reflections

Three studies informed the reflections in this chapter: a study exploring *the home and school literacy practices interface in rural Zimbabwe* (Ngwaru, 2010), a study evaluating the *East Africa Quality in Early Learning* (EAQEL) project in Kenya and Uganda (Ngwaru & Njoroge, 2011), and a study examining *early literacy development for sustainable schooling in Southern Tanzania* (Ngwaru et al., 2013).

Home and School Literacy Practices Interface in Rural Zimbabwe Study. This study used a qualitative research design involving home and school observations, interviews, focus group discussions with parents and teachers, and analysis of professional documents in the school, such as teacher scheme and plan books, pupil exercise books, class story and text books, and any other relevant records. For this study, interviews and focus group discussions created unique opportunities to listen to teachers and parents voicing their own interpretations and thoughts as well as their frustrations with regard to children's education rather than relying solely on "outsider" interpretations. In other words, participants were encouraged to tell, and did tell, their side of the story in their own words. The study looked at literacy practices at home and school in a more homogeneous rural setting with a particular focus on ten parents from six families and their combined total of 25 primary school–going children. From the school, seven teachers, including student teachers, participated. Slightly more than halfway into the project, sensitization sessions were held with parents and teachers around effective parenting, including increasing dialogue and appreciation between parents and children, constructivist pedagogies, and recognition of children's sociocultural funds of knowledge, respectively. At a joint teacher, parent, and children meeting, both teachers and parents realized how much they needed to work together and pledged the same.

Among the findings, as discussed in some detail later in this chapter, were the following: parents were not aware of the roles they could play in the literacy development of their children; teachers were under the mistaken perception that parents did not know anything about children's literacy development and therefore could not participate in their development either at home or at school; and both parents and teachers perceived literacy development from the Western schooling perspective of reading books and writing for school purposes. Furthermore, teachers' pedagogies completely excluded children's sociocultural funds of knowledge (Moll & Greenberg, 1990).

East Africa Quality in Early Learning (EAQEL) Study. The EAQEL study was an evaluation of a pedagogical intervention based on Rose and Acevedo's (2006) instructional approach to scaffolding literacy instruction—"*Reading to Learn*" (RtL)—a systematic approach to the teaching of reading and math developed and first used in Australia but adapted to different educational contexts around the world to recognize local pedagogical rhythms. RtL provides a systematic and explicit approach to the teaching of reading and math to enable all children to succeed by breaking complex tasks down to manageable components. In Kenya and Uganda, the intervention was introduced in 115 schools—64 and 51 in Kenya and Uganda, respectively. It involved three strands: (a) training and supporting 115 head teachers (and their deputies) and 345 lower primary teachers (Standard One to Three), 60% of whom were female, to teach literacy and numeracy using the RtL approach; (b) introducing classroom libraries in each of the intervention schools; and (c) introducing, in half of the intervention schools, the Reading for Children (RfC) component where village libraries were initiated to encourage parental involvement in support of their children's education. The evaluation focused on assessing the effectiveness of each of the strands, with specific emphasis on factors that seemed to influence children's reading abilities and acquisition of reading skills. The study equally focused on the learning environment, including availability and utilization of teaching and learning materials and parental involvement at home and in the school. Classroom observations were employed to obtain data on the use of the RtL and the classroom libraries, while interviews, focus group discussions, and analysis of teachers' professional records were important sources of additional information.

The main finding from the study was that although pedagogical interventions were introduced to improve the teaching and learning of literacy and math, there were significant barriers to the attainment of intervention goals. Most significant among the challenges were teachers' inability to use constructivist pedagogies or to develop and use effective teaching learning materials, even when these were available, and the dearth of reading materials. Teachers were inevitably left as the only source of knowledge in the classroom as parents did not participate or engage and were not expected to do so. However, these communities still were endowed with resilience, skills, and knowledge based on their cultural ways of knowing that enabled them to make the best of their situations, as further illustrated below when the RtL intervention project in Kenya successfully trained some parents to run community libraries and RfC programs. These programs made parents so much more aware of the importance of early literacy development that they asked their older, secondary school children to teach them to read so they, in turn, could teach children in preschool and the early grades to read. This demonstrates that with systematic empowerment, these families were ready and capable to embrace effective school-type literacy practices.

Parent–Teacher Empowerment and Early Literacy Development Study. This was a baseline study of literacy development indices in Lindi Rural District of Southern Tanzania based on a sequential mixed method research design to harness the generalizability of surveys and the detailed nature of interpretive data from qualitative methodology. It used a questionnaire survey accompanied by rapid ethnographic observations and interviews, followed by detailed case studies of schools and communities. It was carried out in 86 of 113 primary schools in one rural district representing all schools with preschool sections and involving 276 preschool and lower primary school teachers and 288 parents of children from the same level. The study focused on understanding factors that determine literacy development in low-resourced communities in order to empower parents and teachers for children's sustainable schooling and learning outcomes in Southern Tanzania.

The study was informed primarily by the need to document, through survey and ethnographic procedures, the factors that influenced early literacy development among the 3- to 8-year-olds in rural low-resourced communities in Lindi Rural District of Southern Tanzania. The literacy development perspectives that informed the study blended Africentric perspectives (Nsamenang & Tchombe, 2011; Pence & Nsamenang, 2008) and Eurocentric sociocultural theories such as Vygotsky (1978). This study aimed to contribute knowledge about the influence of participants' socioeconomic and cultural well-being on their children's literacy development in general and school literacy in particular. The goal was to determine possible pedagogical approaches and practices that would speak adequately to the experiences of rural parents and their young children to repudiate marginalization (Ada, 1988; Dei & Asgharzadeh, 2005). It was also informed as much by the need to target parents unable to support their children and unaware of the potency of their involvement in children's literacy development (Ngwaru, 2010; Ngwaru & Njoroge, 2011) as it was by the need to sensitize preschool and early grade teachers who required support in constructive developmental pedagogy (Magolda, 1999).

The study recognized the fact that knowledge is coconstructed by the child and others within the family and the school (McNaughton, 2001). Because much literacy learning takes place in families, homes, and neighborhoods, it is imperative for schools to harness the power of out-of-school learning, especially for children who are at risk (Nickse & Speicher, 1988). The overarching goals were to bridge the gaps between pedagogies influenced by dominant relations of power and those emanating from sociocultural and critical constructivist perspectives.

The questionnaire survey indicated that socioeconomic well-being, in particular the level of their parents' education and income, were major factors influencing the lack of literacy development of children. The parent profiles data clarified this factor further by indicating that the majority (81%) reported their highest level of education as primary school and primary source of income as farming (88%), with the vast majority living on about a dollar a day. It was still the case, however, that their homes were endowed with sociocultural funds of knowledge that would enable them promote their children's learning if they were empowered. The homes were furnished with basic but appropriate items including locally made furniture—beds, chairs, tables, and stools, as well as other paraphernalia for household uses. Some of the furniture gadgetry included coconut flesh extracting devices (mbuzi), spice miniature mortars and pestles, mixers, and special charcoal stoves, as well as decorations and cultural and religious artifacts significant in the lives of the villagers.

Case study data indicated that the target institutions—the schools and communities—had historical, economic, and sociocultural conditions that did not reinforce the link between activities of reading and writing and social structures. The communities were preoccupied with different levels of livelihood challenges, including lack of development, intergenerational poverty, and lack of gainful employment opportunities for their women and youths, all of which could not be solved by the education offered in the schools. They perceived their sociocultural economies as more reliable for their livelihoods than school education because at least they had relied on these economies for generations. This left parents less motivated to encourage their children to pursue school educational goals. Parents openly disparaged school education in its current form as having failed to change their fortunes since even the few whose children had completed "O" Level had nothing to show for it, they said. It was no surprise that they had become cynical about school education because it did not appear to have delivered anybody they knew from the cycle of poverty. This made them further lose trust in civic institutions again because they had proved over the years to be partisan and partial. At one of the case schools, teachers reported and the education officers confirmed that parents were known to be openly hostile to the school agenda because it burdened them to look for secondary school fees and other requirements. These parents echoed Nsamenang and Tchombe's (2011) critique that school education was not automatically bringing economic growth and societal development in Africa, contrary to what was predicted by human capital theory (Dasen & Akkari, 2008). If anything, it was just an inconvenience—taking away children from home and depriving them of meaningful economic activities such as farming and fishing (these were coastal communities). On the other hand, schools were perennially grappling with a range of systemic challenges such as the lack of resources, including inadequate number of teachers, lack of timely responses to their needs by responsible authorities, lack of support from parents and communities, and lack of motivation among children.

The study underscored the need for genuine efforts to uplift communities from their current political economies. The appropriate starting point for the government and development partners was to make an effort to understand the deep-rooted factors that made these communities culturally vibrant and cohesive. This is where development advocates had to begin if they were to endear themselves to the target populations. Initiatives such as schooling had to be seen to be part of the cultural improvement trajectories of local communities. The local population perceived that schooling had transformed other communities in different contexts but would not necessarily transform their own. Many indications pointed to the lack of cohesion between factors that could positively promote literacy development and local political economies. Communities appeared to miss genuine agency in current socioeconomic structures, including school education and modern political governance.

For immediate and medium-term turnaround, community development projects needed to align themselves with local social-cultural ways of knowing. Curran (1984) asserts that Africa "provides opportunities for learning and development which simply do not exist in the West and therefore are not considered by the predominant theories" (p. 4). Literacy learning at home, as abundantly recorded in African literature (e.g., Achebe, 1958; Kenyatta, 1939) to be socioculturally based, should become part of the school curriculum. Literacy development as currently conceived to constitute only school education should be reconsidered. The curriculum, teachers, and schools need to be primed to adopt the sociocultural view of literacy that would smoothly merge home and family experiences into the school curriculum. This would go a long way to make schooling an institution that can transform communities.

The Need to Invest in Parents' Empowerment

In most African countries, children from low-income families grow up in environments where parental involvement in their education is either minimal or absent. Low-income parents often do not see beyond their economic circumstances. The three studies informing the reflections in this chapter highlighted some of the contextual reasons why parents cannot participate in the literacy development of their children and why their homes can be described as lacking in intellectual motivation and reading opportunities (Ngwaru, 2010).

It must be noted that intellectual motivation and even reading opportunities are not necessarily viewed from a Western perspective. In Zimbabwe, parents were more often than not preoccupied with poverty, socioeconomic insecurity, morbidity (usually arising from the scourge of HIV/AIDS), and a lack of understanding of the potency of their involvement. In Kenya, it was the same preoccupation with poverty and lack of education that left some parents thinking that since they could not read themselves, they could not help their children. These were parents' ruling passions (Barton & Hamilton, 1998)—that is, their immediate priorities—that made them appear not to place a high value on the educational and intellectual achievements of their children, as if they believed that school education was not for them. It was always the case however that parents in all the countries expressed satisfaction at the roles they played at home—looking after younger siblings, taking charge of cattle and chickens, as well as domestic chores. At a practical level, parents were doing everything in their power to help their children acquire a well-rounded education from home to school. Parents reported, in a manner seemingly evoking Maslow's (1943) hierarchy of needs, that direct participation or involvement in school activities was likely to occur only after their families' physiological needs of hunger, thirst, and bodily discomfort had been satisfied.

In a focus group discussion, one parent in the Zimbabwe study, Mr. Mhosva (all names used are pseudonyms), said: "I know you want us to talk about the education of our children, but you will appreciate why we want to tell you about our problems so that at least you know the challenges we face every day" (Ngwaru, 2010, p. 85). He continued:

> I live with my wife and children and I am not in good health at all; my wife has lots of problems coping with domestic and household chores and work in the fields without as much support from me as used to be the case when we were both fit and healthy. Perhaps I am HIV positive—I don't know—but I suffer pains in the chest and have frequent severe heartburn. This is part of the reason we leave the education of the children to teachers. (p. 90)

In this Zimbabwean community, as in others throughout Africa, disease, poverty, and the resultant mortality are everyday realities and it is an illusion to believe that, left on their own, parents in these circumstances can prioritize their children's literacy development. What makes the need for advocacy and empowerment particularly poignant is that families often do not have the means to make their way out of their difficult situations. For instance, Mr. Mhosva, focusing on the stewardship of the land, underlined the causes of food insecurity:

> Our fields are now sandy and require fertilizers or organic manure but we have none because our government cannot give us agricultural inputs and our cattle are depleted. There does not seem to be an easy way out of this quandary because we have no means to pull ourselves out of this on our own ... (quoted in Ngwaru, 2010, p. 88)

About the way they perceived their role in the education of their children, another participant, Mr. Madzibaba, highlighted how they nevertheless still contributed to their children's education. They ensured, as far as possible, that children's everyday needs were satisfied as a way of helping them to remain in school. They provided adequate food and appropriate clothing, and struggled to pay school fees. In Zimbabwe, school fees entitle children to school books and stationery and those with arrears do not receive any learning materials but instead are periodically sent home to force their parents to pay. Not only does this practice make children disaffected, it also encourages them to drop out and leave parents frustrated.

A third participant, Mrs. Gato, was a widow living with four dependants—her 15-year-old daughter (a secondary school pupil at the time) as well as two sons and a nephew, all attending primary school. Like many other homes in the Zimbabwe community study, Mrs. Gato's home comprised two simple and basic round huts under thatch without any other buildings. Despite the obvious poverty, and despite the absence of most Western-type intellectual stimulation or books, Mrs. Gato's home still had an abundance of wealth, the efficacy of which she was unaware of. This wealth took the form of oral histories, family stories, and real-life experiences that could have been used to help children better understand the context of their lives and situations. For example, enduring extended family ties existed between her family and that of her father-in-law who had lent them a small herd of cattle for domestic purposes, including their milk needs. These were resources equivalent in complexity to any other in other cultures that could be used as part of the social-cultural resources for literacy development. Generally, the homes did not have the culture of reading or resources in the mold of books, paper, or pencils; they had practical implements for everyday livelihoods in rural contexts. Unfortunately, these were not used to enhance literacy development because the parents were not aware. After sensitization and empowerment meetings about the need to ensure that parenting brought about children's social-emotional development, family harmony, and literacy development, Mrs. Gato said:

> From this study ..., I learnt quite a lot about all that. I did not know how to handle my children; we could not go on well together. I didn't know (1) when to assign them on the different home errands needing attention, (2) when to get them doing household chores and (3) when to get them to do their homework or something related to their school work. I didn't realize at all that I could actually help my children with their homework after school. I always thought it was the responsibility of the school teachers. I now realize that with this kind of knowledge I can bring up my children in a much better way than those families with both parents. (Ngwaru, 2010, p. 93)

In Southern Tanzania, in Lindi Rural District, cultural resources were even more abundant. The region was a rich coastal area with tropical crops and food resources. Cassava, yams, and coconuts formed an important part of the people's diet. As depicted in Figure 4.1, young girls led by the elder ones prepare the staple food as part of everyday home chores done collaboratively in play mood.

In Figure 4.1, seven girls and two boys are supporting the elder girl as she pounds the staple cassava (*mihogo*) using mortar, pestle, and a reed

Figure 4.1. Traditional Food Processing in a Village of Southern Tanzania

tray (*wanatumia kinu namuti wake wakiweka kwenye ungo*). Each one of the girls learns in that natural context while the boys are looking after the goats (only one in the figure) but obviously supporting the processing. These examples of growing up together, learning cooperatively, and supporting each other form the basis of child development dovetailed to cultural, social, and economic production. These are abundant funds of knowledge that can be utilized even in the development of school literacy.

Recognizing Family Funds of Knowledge

Any intervention to mitigate the literacy development challenges facing parents in low-resourced settings requires the acknowledgement and utilization of families' funds of knowledge—those historically developed and accumulated strategies, skills, abilities, ideas, practices, and bodies of knowledge that are essential to a household's functioning and well-being (Gonzalez et al., 1993). Most villagers in the Zimbabwe and Tanzania communities, for instance, had skills which allowed them to provide piecemeal labor and earn income locally. In Zimbabwe, the community as a whole drew on a wide variety of practical skills and relationships relevant to their context, such as crop and animal husbandry, treating cattle diseases with traditional herbs and methods, sinking deep wells, basketry, and reed mat-weaving, as well as carving tools and implements such as mortars and pestles. In Tanzania, communities had similar skills as they depended on growing cashew and coconuts as well as fishing. The income from these activities, however, was always insufficient for their annual needs (see Chapter 3 by Ng'asike for another example of local funds of knowledge relevant to early educational curriculum for children of a rural African community).

Teachers in both countries seldom mentioned any of these examples in their classrooms because local teachers thought that this kind of knowledge was not part of the "correct" curriculum. Teachers did not realize that homes of the low-resourced still had abundant worthwhile knowledge that could become a rich source of curriculum material. Culturally appropriate literacy development materials for the home and school could be developed from such knowledge, skills, experiences, and relationships if teachers were empowered to embrace the concept. The view of this chapter is that stakeholders of literacy should hold this positive and realistic sociocultural view that low-income households contain ample cultural and cognitive resources with great potential for classroom instruction (Moll & Greenberg, 1990; Moll et al., 1990). Unfortunately, this view contrasted sharply with the study families' prevailing perceptions (and those of working class and rural families in general) of local cultural resources as socially disorganized and intellectually deficient. Sadly, these perceptions, rather than being challenged, are reinforced by the dominant forces of power behind schooling and other social programs. This is the reason why parents think the way they do and need to be made aware of the efficacy of the abundant funds of knowledge in their local contexts. They need to embrace this to groom their children and develop them emotionally in preparation for lifelong literacy development.

It was not a coincidence that the clearest commonality across the three studies was parents' lack of awareness about how they could contribute toward their children's literacy development. This was most regrettable given that the contexts in which they were raising their children possessed local funds of knowledge that remained untapped in the absence of their empowerment. In Kenya, at the onset of a pedagogical intervention, parents refused to volunteer to take part in the running of village libraries, saying they had no skills to offer and in some cases could not read themselves (Ngwaru & Njoroge, 2011). After being empowered through project training, however, they were surprised by their effectiveness when many children became inspired as their parents took charge of their reading. The following testimony by one community librarian underscores this point:

> I discovered that learning to read was such an important skill [that] I could not trust anyone to do it for my children. I am satisfied with the progress my Standard Two and Four children are making in reading because when they come from school they come here to the community library and I continue with them. (Ngwaru & Njoroge, 2011, p. 45)

What was even more significant about this study was that reading with children supported children's social-emotional development, with children expressing feelings of satisfaction and encouragement after realizing that home and school were on the same continuum. Both parents and children said that their relationships had improved tremendously through the close cooperation arising from the RfC program. Similar findings emerged from the Zimbabwe study where:

> At the outset, parents perceived that they had no role to play in the formal schooling of their children, believing that this was the sole responsibility of the school. Similarly, the teachers saw parents as having no part to play. The only engagement with parents was through the PTC whose main purpose was purely administrative rather than academic. (Ngwaru, 2010, p. 218)

Parents Creating Literacy-Rich Environments

Parents as caring adults need empowerment to create literacy-rich environments, foster social-emotional stability and self-regulation, as well as promote other skills to prepare their children for sustainable access to schooling. Literacy development begins long before children are introduced to formal instruction in elementary school. Children acquire literacy skills in a variety of ways and at different ages. Early behaviors such as reading from pictures and writing scribbles are an important part of children's literacy development. Social interactions with caring adults, including shared storytelling with consistent exposure to literacy materials, where they are available, will nourish literacy development. Literacy-rich environments offer daily, extended conversations with adults about topics that are meaningful and of interest to children. However, even in the literate Western society, research with kindergarten teachers suggests that about 20% of children entering kindergarten do not yet have the necessary social and emotional skills to be "ready" for school. The U.S. National Scientific Council on the Developing Child (2005) estimates that as many as 30% of very low-income children may not have the necessary social and emotional skills. In Africa, these percentages are three- or four-fold. Yet, early social and emotional development is important both in its own right and because aspects of it facilitate cognitive development. Bloch (2002) highlights the fact that when children are young, the adults around them (parents, other adult caregivers, and preschool teachers) are the most important influences on their social and emotional development. For example, children will have lasting impressions about literacy when they see adults following instructions about how to operate a new cell phone or sharing a familiar story from a community newspaper than when they just see forms of print lying in their environment. As the National Scientific Council on the Developing Child (2005) points out, improved parenting methods that promote literacy development, coupled with high-quality preschool education, can support early development in ways that yield long-term social and emotional benefits. In the African context, literacy-rich environments need not be created from Western conventional books and school-based activities but from the vast sociocultural resources embedded in daily activities in a variety of settings.

Promoting Literacy Practices in Local Environments

It has become clear that when planning interventions in low-resourced communities, such as in rural Zimbabwe and Tanzania, literacy-rich environments do not necessarily have to be based on Western examples of abundant books and parents reading to children. Instead, it has to recognize and utilize local knowledge and resources, and embrace features such as:

- Children surrounded by oral language emanating from family experiences and interactions around resources and artifacts in the home.
- Adults sharing their ideas and feelings and encouraging children to express themselves and ask questions about everyday experiences.
- Children seeing adults using a variety of materials for different purposes, such as purchasing mobile phone credit vouchers, merchandizing, or learning about the news.
- Where book and print materials are available, families should consider children's emergent reading and writing to be real, valuable experiences. They should accept children's efforts without correcting mistakes or providing direct instruction.
- Families talking with children about the print they see around them and explaining how it provides information (e.g., signs on buses, labels on food and commodity packaging, etc.).

Parents should not have any reason to fail to engage in literacy development except for lack of awareness. As has been noted, without appropriate awareness parents will often think they are unable to nurture their children's literacy and social-emotional development. Often they begin to think that it is the responsibility of school teachers or those parents in better financial circumstances. It was however illustrated that this could change if they were sensitized. Parents realized that they could still play a big role in their children's literacy development through activities such as finding time to sit with their children and talk about everyday experiences (including their school work), opening any print materials that might be available, telling stories around pictures, and encouraging children to read and feel relaxed with print materials.

Policy Recommendations

With the research-based knowledge we now possess as educationalists and ECCE activists, it is no longer defensible to leave children without carefully planned literacy development programs connecting home and school. Governments in SSA should prioritize policy on ECCE going forward. Boyd, Barnett, Bodrova, Leong, and Gomby (2005) emphasize that policymakers must invest in programs that support development of the whole child, including academic, social, and emotional skills, because these skills reinforce each other. Emphasis should start at the school level, with teachers encouraging parental participation in the form of storytelling as well as interest in their children's play and reading at school and at home.

One of the most cost-effective measures will be school-based sensitization of parents and teachers about the importance of parental involvement and the utilization of children's sociocultural funds of knowledge for lifelong literacy development. It was clear that school curriculum experiences, pedagogy, and materials needed to be aligned to children's family and home cultural knowledge to ensure that parents and communities viewed them to be enhancing their livelihoods. While parents and teachers require empowerment, the school curriculum, especially content and methods of teaching, also urgently requires appropriate adjustment.

Conclusion

The EFA Global Monitoring Report (UNESCO, 2008) indicates that Sub-Saharan Africa has the most negative statistics on indicators of poverty, school dropout rates, gender inequalities in school, incidence of HIV and AIDS, and so on. All these are not likely to go away soon but working toward their reduction and complete reversal can begin now. One cost-effective place to start is ECCE. Children are not only the future of the world, but educated children are indeed the guarantors of a future that can ensure that the subregion will compare favorably to other regions of the world. Children's ability to learn and to function as contributing members of society rests heavily on their development of social competency and emotional health. Clearly, home and family early literacy development together with preschool programs with contextually relevant standards of quality will contribute substantially to this development. The research informing this chapter points to an urgent need to promote better home and family literacy development programs that will lead to equitable preschool access and a fair chance for sustained participation in schooling.

References

Achebe, C. (1958). *Things fall apart*. London, UK: Heinemann.
Ada, A. (1988). Creative reading: A relevant methodology for language minority children. In L. M. Malave (Ed.), *Theory, research and application: Selected papers* (pp. 97–111). Buffalo: Buffalo State University New York.
Barton, D., & Hamilton, M. (1998). *Local literacies. Reading and writing in one community*. New York, NY: Routledge.

Bloch, C. (2002). Building bridges between oral and written language. In N. Alexander (Ed.), *Mother tongue based bilingual education in southern Africa: The dynamics of implementation* (pp. 69–82). Cape Town, SA: PRAESA.
Boyd, J., Barnett, W. S., Bodrova, E., Leong, D. J., & Gomby, D. (2005). *Promoting children's social and emotional development through preschool education* (Preschool Policy Brief, Report No. 7). New Brunswick, NJ: Rutgers, The State University of New Jersey, National Institute for Early Educational Research (NIEER).
Colette, C. (2008). *Accelerating early grades reading in high priority EFA countries: A desk review.* Supported by the EQUIP1 project, American Institutes for Research.
Curran, H. V. (1984). Introduction. In H. V. Curran (Ed.), *Nigerian children: Developmental perspectives* (pp. 1–11). London, UK: Routledge & Kegan Paul.
Dasen, P. R., & Akkari, A. (2008). Introduction: Ethnocentrism in education and how to overcome it. In P. R. Dasen & A. Akkari (Eds.), *Educational theories and practices from the "majority world"* (pp. 7–22). New Delhi, India: Sage.
Dei, G., & Asgharzadeh, A. (2005). Language, education and development: Case studies from southern contexts. *Language and Education, 17*(6), 421–449.
Gonzalez, N., Moll, L. C., Floyd-Tenery, M., Rivera, A., Rendon, P., Gonzales, R., & Amandi, C. (1993). *Funds of knowledge: Learning from language minority households.* Washington, DC: National Centre for Research on Cultural Diversity and Second Language Learning.
Karoly, L. A., Kilburn, M. R., & Cannon, J. (2005). *Proven benefits of early childhood interventions* (Rand Corporation Research Brief, RB-9145 PNC). Retrieved from http://www.rand.org/pubs/research_briefs/RB9145.html
Kenyatta, J. (1939). *Facing Mount Kenya.* London, UK: Secker and Warburg. (Mercury Edition, 1961)
Magolda, B. M. B. (1999). *Creating contexts for learning and self-authorship: Constructive-developmental pedagogy* (Vanderbilt Issues in Higher Education). Nashville, TN: Vanderbilt University Press.
Maslow, A. (1943). A theory of human motivation. *Psychological Review, 50,* 370–396.
McNaughton, S. (2001). Co-constructing expertise: The development of parents' and teachers' ideas about literacy practices and the transition to school. *Journal of Early Childhood Literacy, 1*(1), 40–58.
Moll, L. C., & Greenberg, J. B. (1990). Creating zones of possibilities: Combining social contexts for instruction. In L. C. Moll (Ed.), *Vygotsky and education: Instructional implications and applications for socio-historical psychology* (pp. 319–348). Cambridge, UK: Cambridge University Press.
Moll, L. C., Velez-Ibanez, C., Greenberg, J., Whitmore, K., Saavedra, E., Dworin, J., & Andrade, R. (1990). *Community knowledge and classroom practice: Combining resources for literacy instruction.* Tucson: University of Arizona College of Education and Bureau of Applied Research in Anthropology.
National Scientific Council on the Developing Child. (2005). *Young children develop in an environment of relationships* (Working Paper No. 1). Retrieved from http://developingchild.harvard.edu/resources/reports_and_working_papers/working_papers/wp1/
Ngwaru, J. M. (2010). *Literacy practices at home and school for rural children in Zimbabwe: The real pedagogical dilemmas.* Dudweiler Landstr, Germany: VDM Verlag.
Ngwaru, J. M., Mweru, M., & Oluga, M. (2013). *Early literacy development for sustainable schooling in Southern Tanzania* (Interim results). Unpublished paper, Institute for Educational Development, Aga Khan University, Tanzania.
Ngwaru, J. M., & Njoroge, L. (2011). *East Africa Quality in Early Learning (EAQEL) Program.* Evaluation Study Report for Aga Khan Foundation by Aga Khan University, Institute for Educational Development, East Africa.
Nickse, R., & Speicher, N. A. (1988). An intergenerational adult literacy project: A family intervention/prevention model. *Journal of Reading, 31,* 364–642.

Nsamenang, B., & Tchombe, M. S. (Eds.). (2011). *Handbook of African educational theories and practices: A generative teacher education curriculum*. Bamenda, Cameroon: Human Development Research Centre.

Pence, A., & Nsamenang, A. B. (2008). *A case for ECD in Africa* (Bernard van Leer Foundation Working Paper No. 51). The Hague, Netherlands: Bernard van Leer Foundation.

Reynolds, A., Wang, M., & Walberg, H. (Eds.). (2003). *Early childhood programs for a new century*. Washington, DC: CWLA Press.

Rose, D., & Acevedo, C. (2006). Designing literacy in-servicing: Learning to read: Reading to learn. Proceedings of the Australian Systemic Functional Linguistics Conference (2006), University of New England. In R. Ruddell & H. Singer (Eds.), *Theoretical models and processes of reading* (4th ed., pp. 83–103). Newark, DE: International Reading Association.

UNESCO. (1990). *The World Declaration on Education for All, World Conference on Education for All: Meeting basic needs*. Jomtien, Thailand: Author.

UNESCO. (2000). *World Education Forum*. Dakar, Senegal, April 26–28.

UNESCO. (2008). *Education for all: Global monitoring report*. Paris, France: UNESCO.

UNESCO. (2010). *Reaching the marginalized* (EFA Global Monitoring Report 2010). Paris, France: UNESCO. Retrieved from unesdoc.unesco.org/images/0018/001866/186606E.pdf

UWEZO Tanzania. (2011). *Are our children learning?* (Annual Learning Assessment Report). Uwezo, Tenmet, & Hivos/Taweza. Retrieved from http://twaweza.org/uploads/files/ALA_UWEZO.pdf

Vygotsky, L. (1978). *Mind in society: The development of higher psychological processes*. Cambridge, MA: Harvard University Press.

Zigler, E. F., Gilliam, W. S., & Jones, S. (Eds.). (2006). *A vision for universal preschool education*. Cambridge, MA: Cambridge University Press.

JACOB MARRIOTE NGWARU is a lecturer at the Institute for Educational Development, Aga Khan University, Dar es Salaam, Tanzania.

Matafwali, B., & Serpell, R. (2014). Design and validation of assessment tests for young children in Zambia. In R. Serpell & K. Marfo (Eds.), *Child development in Africa: Views from inside. New Directions for Child and Adolescent Development, 146*, 77–96.

5

Design and Validation of Assessment Tests for Young Children in Zambia

Beatrice Matafwali, Robert Serpell

Abstract

Early childhood education has received unprecedented attention among African policymakers in recent years, recognizing that the early years form an important foundation upon which later development is anchored and noting evidence that various Early Childhood Development (ECD) indicators are predictive of future academic success. Central to the provision of quality early childhood education is assessment of developmental outcomes. But currently there is little systematic documentation of culturally appropriate child assessment instruments in Africa. We briefly review the literature on cross-cultural issues in child assessment and identify a variety of approaches to test design and adaptation. We then describe the process through which two child assessment instruments were developed in the Zambian context and empirical evidence was collected of their ecocultural and psychometric validity: the Panga Munthu Test and the Zambia Child Assessment Tool (ZamCAT). Implications are derived from these examples for future development of culturally responsive child assessment instruments in Africa. © 2014 Wiley Periodicals, Inc.

Assessment of children in the early stages of development has become a focus of interest among educational practitioners in Sub-Saharan Africa due to growing recognition of the importance of early intervention to improve children's overall development and to enhance their educational outcomes. Early intervention includes an array of services provided to children and their mothers in the period from conception to the beginning of formal schooling. Longitudinal studies in the United States and the United Kingdom have demonstrated that such intervention impacts positively on developmental outcomes in all domains including language, cognitive, socioemotional, interpersonal, and motor functions (Denton & McPhee, 2009; Sylva, Melhuish, Sammons, Siraj-Blatchford, & Taggart, 2011). In East Africa, a study by Mwaura, Sylva, and Malmberg (2008) revealed that children from impoverished backgrounds who attended early childhood education (ECE) attained better developmental outcomes.

In the Zambian Early Childhood Development Project, Zuilkowski, Fink, Moucheraud, and Matafwali (2012) found that participation in ECE does not only improve academic outcomes but also encourages a timely enrollment of children into Grade 1. It is possible that parents whose children have been exposed to ECE are motivated to enroll their children in Grade 1 on time by their interpretation of their children's participation in school-related activities as evidence of school readiness.

Several complementary functions can be served by systematic assessment of young children in Africa as elsewhere. These include population level detection of children at risk for disability and/or with special educational needs, differential diagnosis of conditions affecting optimal development, individualized intervention program planning, monitoring of developmental progress, evaluation of programs, and research on any of these topics.

Research to document the processes through which children exposed to ECE achieve superior developmental outcomes demands attention to their competencies in various domains and to the growth of those competencies over the course of development. The history of research on the impact of Head Start programs in the context of the War on Poverty in the United States shows that measurement can be a contentious issue, with some researchers claiming large and significant gains from enrollment, while others found that such gains were short-lived (Zigler & Finn-Stevenson, 1992). ECE services afford an important opportunity to detect children at risk for developmental disability with a view to offering them compensatory special education (Mitchell & Brown, 1991). But identifying a child as eligible for special education tends to be a somewhat haphazard process in Sub-Saharan Africa, where specialized assessment services are rare. Moreover, even when systematic assessment is undertaken by professionals (e.g., in Zimbabwe; Mpofu & Nyanungo, 1998), hardly any of the tests in use have been subjected to any systematic restandardization on the local population. In order for ECE to fulfill its potential for social benefits, there is a need for reliable and valid measures of children's development. Documentation of child assessment tests in the African region remains fragmented (Serpell, 1999). This has hampered the accuracy of individual assessments and consequently the generation of reliable estimates of prevalence of childhood disabilities in Sub-Saharan Africa (Durkin & Maenner, 2014; Fryers, 1986; Schuurman, 1995; Serpell & Jere-Folotiya, 2011). Many documents on the Internet claiming an official status about health and education in African countries project inappropriate foreign statistics or unwarranted global generalizations as the basis for specific numerical estimates of the nation's children with various types of disability.

From what we have observed, the use of standardized tests of Western origin to measure developmental outcomes among children in Sub-Saharan Africa is very widespread and is often justified on the grounds that no more culturally appropriate assessment instruments are available. However, doing so runs the risk of seriously misrepresenting the level of functioning of African children. Research has shown that importation of tests to non-Western contexts can be a source of unfairness (Greenfield, 1997; Nampijja et al., 2010; Nell, 2000; Serpell, 1988; Serpell & Haynes, 2004). The use of measures of Western origin in the assessment of children from diverse cultural groups is subject to biases arising from children's lack of familiarity with test demands and poor translation of test items (Ardila & Roselli, 2003; Wicherts, Dolan, Carlson, & van der Maas, 2010). Even where efforts have been made to develop instruments more appropriate for Sub-Saharan Africa, there remains a challenge of carefully selecting appropriate test items and systematic validation of assessment items to ensure responsiveness to cultural and linguistic diversity within the local context. In this chapter, we highlight salient features involved in the design and validation of assessment instruments to ensure local relevance. First, we summarize the challenges arising from the application of Western developed instruments. Then we provide a detailed account of two assessment measures that have been developed in Zambia, the Panga Munthu Test (PMT) and the Zambia Child Assessment Test (ZamCAT), drawing attention to methods applied in the processes of design, refinement, and validation.

Cross-Cultural Issues in Child Assessment

A classic issue in cross-cultural psychology has been the difference between nominal and functional equivalence. "If similar activities have different functions in different societies, their parameters cannot be used for comparative purposes" (Frijda & Jahoda, 1966, p. 116). "If we know that the meaning of a given objectively defined (i.e., nominally equivalent) behaviour is different in culture A than in culture B, then a difference between the groups A and B in the frequency or intensity with which the behaviour is manifested should not be interpreted in terms of only one culture's meaning for that behaviour" (Serpell, 1990, p. 110). This basic principle has been applied to the evaluation of tests in terms of bias. Van de Vijver and associates consider that bias occurs when score differences in the indicators of a particular construct do not correspond with differences in the underlying trait or ability. They identify three types of bias, namely construct bias, method bias, and content bias also known as item bias. "Construct bias is likely to appear when test authors from various societies use definitions of the concept under study that do not fully overlap. *Method bias* occurs when a cultural factor that is not relevant to the construct studied affects most or all items of a test in a differential way across the cultures studied" (Van de Vijver & Poortinga, 1997, p. 30).

The third type of bias is embedded in technical aspects of psychometrics and includes departures from structural equivalence and full-score equivalence (Van de Vijver, 2002). These questions pertain to cross-cultural comparison using the same or closely cognate instruments. In the case studies of test development in Zambia presented in this chapter, we focus on strategies for avoiding construct bias and method bias in the design and standardization of tests for use within a given society. Although confining the project to a single society might seem to bypass issues of cross-cultural bias, cultural variations also arise within a society, raising the possibility that a locally developed test might discriminate unfairly between groups within that society that differ in respect of cultural characteristics such as language or parental education.

With regard to the construct of intelligence, Hilliard (1975) noted that "it is likely that contextual observations of children functioning cognitively in regular situations would reveal patterns of intelligence which are systematically missed by standardised measuring situations" (p. 27). Numerous studies have drawn attention to the importance attached in indigenous African cultures to social intelligence, which includes characteristics such as knowing one's role in the family and the ability to deal with socially complicated situations (Dasen et al., 1985; Grigorenko et al., 2001; Serpell, 1977). Even in the United States, such characteristics form part of everyday conceptions of an ideally intelligent person (Sternberg, Conway, Ketron, & Bernstein, 1981), but they are usually not covered by psychometric tests of intelligence. Holding, Abubakar, and Kitsao-Wekulo (2008) observed that Western tests of intelligence emphasize skills such as reasoning, memory, and acquired knowledge, but lack the social component of African conceptualization of intelligence.

Van de Vijver and Tanzer (1997/2004) distinguished three types of method bias: sample bias, administration bias, and instrument bias. Sample bias is due to noncomparability of the sample which may result from confounding factors such as level of education. Standardization of tests for use with the school-age population in countries where universal enrollment is mandated by law includes only children enrolled in school. But in many African countries, due to insufficient educational provision, as well as circumstances such as extreme poverty or displacement by civil war, significant numbers of children of school age attend school irregularly or not at all. There is considerable evidence that exposure to formal schooling leads to improved performance on tests of cognitive functioning in specific domains such as language, attention, memory, and phonological awareness (Rogoff, 1981; Serpell & Hatano, 1997). Alcock, Holding, Mung'ala-Odera, and Newton (2008) found a significant correlation between cognitive abilities and the number of years of a child's schooling in Eastern Kenya. They therefore cautioned that where a standardized test of cognitive abilities is being designed for a population that includes large numbers of children who do not attend school, the ideal approach would be to standardize the test separately for children in school and those out of school, so as to avoid misdiagnosis of cognitive impairments in children with limited school experience.

Instrument bias usually occurs when test stimuli are not familiar to the child. Okonji (1971) compared the performance of Nigerian and British children on sorting objects and animal models. The study found different levels of categorical sorting by 6–12-year-old schoolboys depending on the familiarity of the objects to be sorted. Deregowski and Serpell (1971) asked British and Zambian children to sort miniature models of animals and motor vehicles and in another condition to sort photographs of these models. Although no cross-cultural differences were found for sorting the models, the British children obtained higher scores than the Zambian children when photographs were sorted.

Performance on any given cognitive task calls on a variety of skills, some of which develop at similar rates among children in various developmental niches (Super & Harkness, 1986), while others depend on particular types of experience that are distinctive to particular cultural settings. In their natural environments, children of rural African communities engage in self-initiated play activities that reflect a number of aspects of intelligence such as creativity, innovation, cognition, and spatial abilities as a source of pleasure, recreation, and relaxation. These activities involve a different set of abilities from those that are called upon by standardized Western instruments, such as the Koh's Block Design and Bender Gestalt tests (Serpell, 1971).

The ecocultural context of Zambian urban socialization in the 1970s was observed to offer relatively few opportunities or incentives for children to acquire the skills of manipulating blocks or pencils, or of interpreting pictures or diagrams. By contrast, this urban Zambian developmental niche offered relatively more opportunities and incentives for acquiring wire modeling skills than the niche of child development in urban English homes, whereas both niches afforded equal opportunities for children to acquire clay modeling skills. The hypothesis was therefore formulated that each group of children would surpass the other depending on the representational medium in which a pattern reproduction task was presented. An experimental study (Serpell, 1979) provided systematic confirmation: Zambian children outperformed their English counterparts on pattern reproduction in the medium of wire, whereas the English children outperformed their Zambian counterparts when the same patterns were reproduced with pencil and paper.

Cross-cultural differences have also been found on tests requiring pictorial perception. Hudson (1962) compared performance between South African children of African and European heritage on their interpretation of pictorial representation of three-dimensional space. African children demonstrated great difficulty in perceiving depth in these pictures. This finding was replicated with children in several other African countries (Deregowski, 1968; Mundy-Castle, 1966; Omari & MacGinitie, 1974; Opolot, 1976). These authors all concluded that the ability to perceive pictures in three dimensions depends heavily on experience with pictorial materials. A number of studies have shown that the skill of pictorial depth perception can be taught (Deregowski, 1974; Mshelua & Lapidus, 1990). In a Ugandan study, Nampijja et al. (2010) observed that children in higher grades of nursery school performed better in pictorial tasks, vocabulary, and recall skills. Within contemporary African societies, children from more affluent, urban homes consistently score higher than their less privileged peers on Western-type tests of cognitive ability. The effect of parental education on test performance has also been reported within Western societies. Some scholars (Durojaiye, 1984; Vernon, 1969) have interpreted the higher scores of African children exposed to privileged environmental stimulation at home as evidence of higher intelligence inspired by Western cultural influences, while others have argued that they represent highly specific skills and attitudes derived from experience with particular resources embedded in Western cultural practices (Serpell, 2000).

The intuitions of test developers are not always sufficient to eliminate such sources of bias. During the validation of the Child Assessment Tool for Zambia (CDAZ), a screening tool for children aged 0–5 years (Ettling et al., 2006), test items requiring the use of scissors to cut paper were introduced for the assessment of fine motor skills to replace items requiring manipulation of a pencil, on the grounds that many rural Zambian families did not promote drawing by young children and less than 20% of Zambian children were enrolled in formal ECE programs. But the scissors cutting tasks yielded consistently poor performance among young children in rural communities. Further inquiry revealed that many parents in rural households did not allow their young children to play with a pair of scissors for fear of injury, as no plastic scissors suitable for play were available. Another test item required the child to identify a pictorial representation of a cow. In one province many children who successfully identified pictures of other domestic animals referred to this picture as a goat. The research team then realized that keeping cattle was not common in that province and as such, children lacked exposure to the target stimulus. These cases illustrate the value of empirical pilot research in eliminating sources of item bias.

Other procedural features of formal testing may become a source of method bias. Alant, Tesner, and Taljaardt (1992) have observed that "not only do children growing up in socially and educationally disadvantaged environments have a minimal exposure to the more formal language of tests associated with literacy, they also have had little experience of the type of discrete point questioning which may spontaneously emerge from such exposure" (p. 201). Many Western tests place a strict limit on the amount of time allowed for a child to respond to each item, on the supposition that speed of response is indicative of cognitive ability. But it appears likely that merely instructing the testee to respond "as fast as possible" is not sufficient to overcome the tendency for many African children to deliberately take their time to decide on how to respond, perhaps reflecting an emphasis on accuracy over speed in indigenous cultural conceptions of intelligence (Wober, 1974).

Common Approaches to Assessment Test Adaptation

The challenges arising from importation of Western developed assessment tools have created a resource gap for child assessment in Sub-Saharan Africa. If it is not adequately addressed, this is likely to hamper quality service delivery for children. In this section we begin from the premise that while development of a culture-free assessment tool is impossible, there is potential to develop relatively culturally appropriate assessment tools through the application of systematic test development procedures. We present several procedures in development of assessment tests that have been frequently cited in the literature. Serpell (1988) noted that in the absence of local psychometric technology psychologists in the Third World have resorted to a number of alternative strategies including dispensing with tests altogether; adopting various dynamic approaches to evaluating an individual's capacity for learning; using tests imported from another culture, together with *ad hoc* modifications of selected items or criteria based on an intuitive assessment of their cultural inappropriateness; systematically adapting and restandardizing imported tests for local populations; and developing new tests using concepts, methods, and materials derived from local cultures.

Holding et al. (2008) distinguished three broad approaches to test development in Africa: adoption, adaptation, and assembly. Adoption entails direct transfer of an already existing assessment instrument from one cultural context to the other, with modification mainly limited to translation into the target language while maintaining the content and procedures of the original instrument. Although this may seem to be a convenient and affordable option especially in economically constrained environments, the approach has serious shortcomings. The normative standards of the test may be specific to a particular culture and may not be universally applicable. Cultural differences between the original sample and the target sample may induce bias in test measurement. To circumvent this, Abubakar et al. (2007) applied the adaptation approach in development of the Kilifi Developmental Checklist (KDC), a culturally appropriate measure that was successfully employed to evaluate developmental outcomes in children with cerebral malaria. Their study demonstrated that with systematic selection of constructs and measures, development of culturally appropriate instruments to measure developmental outcomes is feasible even in resource-constrained regions like Sub-Saharan Africa.

The process of adapting a test for use in new cultural contexts involves modification of test items, administration instructions, and response options with the aim of producing functional equivalence (Hambleton, 1994). Adaptation is based on the Universalist Model which assumes that child development is universal and comparable across cultures (Herdman, Fox-Rushby, & Badia, 1998). The domain of motor skills may appear to follow a universal developmental trajectory. However, cultural factors may require methodological variation in the assessment of children in this domain. For instance, a test requiring the child to climb a staircase would be inappropriate in a rural African setting where children lack exposure to staircases. In cases where the psychological construct has been clearly defined and maintains a universal sequence, modification of the assessment method may be sufficient to make the instrument suitable in another cultural context. Thus, it is standard practice for an instrument developed and validated with one language group to be translated into the target language when it is applied in another context in order to ensure linguistic equivalence and comparability. While some instructions may be easy to translate faithfully across languages, challenges may arise when the particular phrasing of the instructions in a translated version of the test has unique connotations as this may threaten validity of the instrument.

Assembly involves the construction of an entirely new instrument when existing instruments are deemed inappropriate in the target culture or when the study involves a novel research topic for which no suitable instrument is yet available (Harkness, Van de Vijver, and Johnson, 2003; Holding et al., 2008). This approach takes no interest in performance comparability with other groups.

Analysis of Instrument Design and Validation in Zambia

In this section, we describe the application of two different approaches to test design and validation: systematically adapting and restandardizing imported tests for local populations, with reference to the ZamCAT, an assessment tool for children aged 5–6 years; and developing new tests using concepts, methods, and materials derived from local cultures, with reference to the Panga Munthu Test (PMT), a nonverbal cognitive test for children aged

3–15 years. We have chosen to provide a detailed account of these measures because they have reasonably well-defined diagnostic functions and have been validated on fairly large samples. Another important feature is that the PMT and some components of the ZamCAT are deep rooted in a range of skills that are widely cultivated in African communities across the continent.

Panga Munthu Test (PMT). The *Panga Munthu* (make a person) Test is a nonverbal cognitive test. The motivation for developing this test was to devise a culturally appropriate measure for the assessment of intelligence in Zambian children. The test requires the child to make a model of a human being using clay or plasticine. The model is then scored for accuracy of detail in a manner similar to the scoring key for the Goodenough–Harris Draw-a-person test (DPT; Harris, 1963), which requires the child to draw a person using paper and pencil.

Core features of the test were first designed by Serpell (1974) in response to his dissatisfaction with imported tests as abnormally difficult for urban Zambian children. Based on the evidence of Serpell's (1979) cross-cultural study cited earlier, the first version of the test was designed to detect individual differences in children's pattern reproduction skills in a familiar medium. Clay was chosen over wire for girls since our informal inquiries suggested that a gender bias existed within the current fashion of children's play in Zambia against girls' active participation in building wire cars, and the Zambian girls in our experimental study performed significantly less well than boys on the wire medium task, whereas no gender difference was observed in the medium of clay. A simple 10-point scoring system was devised, based on pilot testing, to generate a numerical index of faithfulness in reproducing key features of a clay mannikin.

This first version of the PMT was administered to a sample of 57 children aged 6–14 years in a rural Chewa community (Kondwelani) in Zambia's Eastern Province in 1973 (Serpell, 1974, 1977) as part of a battery of tests that served as one of several baseline measures for a longitudinal follow-up study (Serpell, 1993). Significant correlations were found with age and with other locally developed tests, but no concordance between the ranking of children on any of the early childhood tests and their ranking in accordance with home village ratings of their intelligence by familiar adults.

Further development and validation of the PMT was conducted by Ezeilo (1978) who extended the scoring system to a 20-point scale including 12 body parts, 7 proportionalities, and 1 point for extra detail. No standard was presented for copying: children were simply instructed to make the best model of a person they could. Independent ratings of 30 models yielded an interrater reliability of .84. Based on analysis of the models created, Ezeilo recommended 5 additional scoring points, bringing the maximum total score to 25. Regarding validity, Ezeilo administered the test to 192 children of normal age for their grade at urban schools catering to low-income neighborhoods. She found a significant steady increase in scores with age, and higher scores by boys than girls, but no significant relation between PMT and teacher ratings of brightness or class marks. In a small clinical sample, children diagnosed as severely impaired in intelligence scored significantly lower on the test than those rated as moderately impaired.

Kathuria and Serpell (1998) extended the standardization to a relatively large sample of 3,231 school-going participants drawn from Grades 1, 3, and 5 at government primary schools in urban and rural areas. Scores on the 25-point scale were significantly correlated with age ($r = .28, p < .001$) and grade ($r = .26, p < .001$), but differences between the two genders or between children in rural and urban ecological zones were not consistently significant. The report presents norms in the form of a five-point scale ranging from low to high for children in each of the three grades, and also for children in three age bands: 7–8, 9–10, and 11–12 years old. Because the records held by African families and schools for children's ages are often unreliable, and the age at which African children first enroll in school tends to be quite variable, the authors recommended that, when assessing an individual, the examiner should consider the child from both angles: stated age and current grade. They emphasized that valid estimates of a child's intelligence should not rely on a single test score, but should reflect a multidimensional profile of the child's performance across a number of settings over a period of time. But the PMT appeared to be "a relatively valid and reliable measure of intellectual functioning in African children of primary school age" (Kathuria & Serpell, 1998, p. 239).

Several subsequent studies have included the 25-point version of PMT as one of several measures, throwing additional light on its psychometric reliability and the nature of the psychological construct that it represents. Serpell (1993) compared performance on the PMT by two Zambian school-going samples, one rural and one urban, who also performed the Goodenough–Harris DPT. Correlations between scores on the two tests were highest among urban boys ($r = .40, N = 41, p < .01$) and lowest among rural girls ($r = -.04, N = 34$, NS). Age was more highly correlated with PMT scores among rural children (boys $r = .65$, girls $r = .66$) than among urban children (boys $r = .47$, girls $r = .24$). Correlations with teacher ratings were generally low for PMT, while for DPT they were higher for boys than for girls. Serpell (1993) concluded that "each of these findings is consistent with the notion that the worlds of home and school are least well integrated psychologically for rural girls and best integrated (in relative terms) for urban boys" (p. 162). With the growth of gender equity in access to schooling in the subsequent three decades, that may no longer be the case.

Matafwali (2005) used the PMT as one of her measures in a study of early literacy development in a sample of 104 third graders drawn from six selected public schools in Lusaka Province. She found a significant correlation between the PMT and blending of sounds ($r = .22, p < .05$) and spelling ($r = .25$, $p < .05$). No gender differences were observed in this sample. However, ecological differences were observed with children from peri-urban schools performing better than those from city schools.

Alcock et al. (2008) included the PMT (giving it the name *Build a Man Test*) in a battery of measures administered to a subset of 38 children drawn from a large representative sample of 6–9-year-olds in a rural area of Eastern Kenya. Eighteen boys and girls who, for various reasons, were not enrolled in school were compared with a group of children, matched for gender and age, who were enrolled in the normally prescribed level of schooling for their age. High levels of interrater reliability (.90) and internal consistency (.82) were found for the PMT, while test–retest reliability after one week was .57. The schooled group performed significantly better than the unschooled group.

Serpell and Jere-Folotiya (2008) analyzed the predictive power of the early, 10-point version of PMT among some of the Kondwelani cohort followed up fourteen years later as young adults with assessments of literacy and numeracy, after completing variable amounts of formal schooling. PMT scores in early childhood were more strongly correlated with number of years of schooling completed and with adult literacy in the local language among the male participants ($r = .44, .43$) than among female participants (.19, .29). Adult ratings of intelligence by village adults familiar with them in early childhood were more predictive of adult literacy for girls (.83, .42) than for boys ($-.27, -.07$). Thus, it appears that the external validity of PMT as a predictor of life-course cognitive outcomes varies according to the educational opportunities open to rural boys and girls. To what extent those predictions were mediated by general cognitive ability remains a matter for further research.

Stemler et al. (2009) reported on a large-scale collaborative study between the University of Zambia and Yale University in the United States, led by Grigorenko from 2003 to 2005, in which PMT was administered alongside the locally developed Zambia academic achievement test (ZAT) and subtests of several American standardized tests of intellectual functioning to a sample of 279 children enrolled in Grades 1–7 at government primary schools in Zambia's Eastern Province or in the city of Lusaka. The principal goal of the study was to establish norms for the ZAT. Internal consistency of PMT scores was .88. PMT scores were consistently more strongly correlated with scores on the local language version of each subtest of the ZAT ($r = .30$ for Math, .32 for Reading Recognition, .24 for Reading Comprehension, and .32 for Pseudo word reading) than with scores on the English language version of the same subtest, where the corresponding correlations were all nonsignificant and close to zero. Thus "it seems that the dimension of cognition tapped by the PMT is closer to that tapped by tests in the children's indigenous language of everyday discourse than to that tapped by tests in the medium of English, which most of them only use at school" (Stemler et al., 2009, p. 190).

Most recently, Ngenda (2011) established the feasibility of using PMT to assess cognitive functioning in children aged 4–6 years with two samples in Zambia's Copperbelt Province, one drawn from an urban preschool and the other from a village community with no preschooling. The construct measured by PMT was explored with two additional tasks designed to tap into complementary dimensions of cognition: a make-a-dog modeling task that shared with PMT the demand for visuomotor coordination in the construction of clay models and a body part name recognition task that shared with PMT the demand for knowledge about the component parts of the human body. Correlations among the scores on these three tasks, age, and ratings of intelligence by a preschool teacher were consistent with theoretical expectations. No significant difference in PMT scores were found between the rural and urban samples, nor between boys and girls. The scores for 5- and 6-year-olds fell within the range designated as normal for 7–8-year-olds in Grade 1 in the tables published by Kathuria and Serpell (1998).

Thus, the 25-point version of PMT has been used in a number of studies with African children and found to be quite reliable. It appears to tap into a cognitive domain that develops equally well in boys and girls in rural and urban populations between the ages of 4 and 12. Its relation with other measures of cognitive functioning suggests that it draws on knowledge about the structure of the human body and visuomotor manipulative skill in the medium of clay, as well as the cognitive function of representation. How this range of competencies relates to measures of academic achievement varies according to how schools teach their students basic subjects such as mathematics and literacy and how the outcomes of that teaching are assessed. While the test samples only a narrow range of the competencies that contribute to what families, schools, and communities consider as intelligence, performance well below the norm on PMT may be a good indicator that a child is at risk for poor performance at school and in other everyday task settings.

Zambia Child Assessment Tool (ZamCAT). The development of ZamCAT was motivated by the desire to document the impact of early childhood experiences on child development in Sub-Saharan Africa. The project spearheaded by the Zambia Early Childhood Project (ZECP) was conceived by Fink of Harvard University. The main objective was to determine the effect of early childhood environment, health, and education on children's development before and through their schooling careers (Fink, Matafwali, Moucheraud & Zuilkowski, 2012). Two major goals were set for the development of an assessment tool for this purpose: to develop an instrument that was sensitive to the local culture and context, and an instrument that is comparable with other international instruments.

The test comprised a broad range of domain areas—language, motor skills, attention and executive functions, nonverbal cognitive skills, and physical growth—carefully selected by a technical committee of Zambian experts with extensive knowledge in child development, special education, and psychology, who were constituted to work with a consultant from Harvard University, Zuilkowski.

Secondly, systematic analysis of subtests that have been extensively used in Africa was done to ensure cultural appropriateness. Specifically, the following core skill areas were selected for inclusion in the ZamCAT: language, fine motor skills, cognitive abilities, and physical growth. Language was measured by subtests from the Peabody Picture Vocabulary Test (PPVT) and a narrative test, while fine motor skills were measured by copying with pencil and paper and fine motor manipulative tasks including placing pebbles on an *nsolo* board (described further later), threading beads, and buttoning a piece of fabric with button holes. Nonverbal cognitive abilities were measured by Block Construction task (a subtest from the Western test of neuropsychological development, NEPSY; Korkman, Kirk, & Kemp, 2007), Pattern Reasoning (a subtest from the Kaufman Assessment Battery for Children, KABC; Kaufman & Kaufman, 2004), Rapid Automatized Naming (RAN), and the Pencil Tapping test (developed and field tested in the Gambia by Jukes & Grigorenko, 2010). Physical growth was indexed by anthropometric measures of height, weight, and Mid Upper Arm Circumference (MUAC). The parent survey captured most of the outcome measures such as socioeconomic status (SES), preschool experience, child health, and maternal health.

The instrument was subjected to translation into the target languages: CiNyanja, IciBemba, SiLozi, ChiTonga, KiKaonde, Lunda, and Luvale. Subsequently, the test was piloted on a sample of 139 children from six provinces. After piloting, the measures were cross-checked for cultural appropriateness and consistency in language use. Subtests such as the Kaufman Pattern Reasoning and NEPSY Block Construction had elicited very low scores, confirming earlier research suggesting that they have a high cultural loading that is biased against the rural Zambian population.

This prompted the development of Tactile Pattern Reasoning, a nonverbal cognitive task (Figure 5.1). Tactile Pattern Reasoning retained the same psychometric construct as Kaufman Pattern Reasoning, but, instead of two-dimensional graphic shapes, the stimulus patterns were constructed from locally familiar materials such as toothpicks, bottle tops, stones, and beads, all of which were distinguishable through both the visual and the tactile modality (Fink et al., 2012). This substitution of solid objects for the pictorial stimuli of the original test appeared to make the task more meaningful to the child and gave rise to a large and significant increase in the number of correct responses (Zuilkowski, Fink, & Matafwali, 2011). Other modifications were made in the light of pilot test results on PPVT where some pictures that were found to be culturally inappropriate were replaced with more culturally relevant items.

The development and validation of the ZamCAT applied the three approaches: adoption, adaptation, and assembly. For instance, in some cases,

Figure 5.1. Dr. Matafwali Demonstrating Tactile Pattern Reasoning Test to a Trainee Assessment Officer

items were applied in their entirety with no modification as was the case with the RAN. Adaptation was done for some items through translation into the target language. Assembly was particularly done in measures of fine motor abilities where a completely new set of subtests was introduced to reduce overreliance on pencil and paper as most of the children in the target sample had limited exposure to preschooling. The test only included a few activities involving pencil and paper. Most importantly, a diverse set of culturally appropriate motor activities available in the child's environment such as bead threading, buttoning, and *nsolo* were included.

Nsolo is an African traditional board game, which is universally known across the indigenous cultural groups within Zambia and also widely known throughout Sub-Saharan Africa, under a variety of different names in different regions (e.g., *bao, mancala, bali, morabaraba, oware*). The *nsolo* board can be created with holes dug in the ground, or carved into a wooden or iron board, and the game is played using pebbles, seeds, or stones as tokens (see Retschitzki, 1988, for further details). This subtest was chosen as an appropriate measure of fine motor skills in ZamCAT because of its cultural familiarity and because it is played by both genders from an early age.

Children were required to place bean seeds in the holes on the 20 cell grid *nsolo* wooden board, and the target behavior was the pincer grip and accuracy in placing the seeds in each cell of the grid.

The refined version of ZamCAT was administered to a sample of 1900 children aged 6 years drawn from six provinces of Zambia (Fink et al., 2012). Results revealed regional disparities in household wealth with the homes of children in the capital city province being wealthier than their counterparts in three predominantly rural provinces. A strong association was found between ECE program enrollment and household wealth: less than 20% of children living in households from the poorest wealth quintiles had attended ECE. Ecological differences were also observed on fine motor scores with children in rural areas scoring an average of 0.15 standard deviations lower than urban children, while only minor gender differences were observed. Interestingly, on the Tactile Pattern Reasoning task rural children scored about 0.28 standard deviations higher than urban children. Gender differences were observed on the RAN test, with urban females scoring on average 0.93 standard deviations higher than urban males.

The study further revealed intercorrelations among subtests. As expected, Tactile Pattern Reasoning correlated highly with Kaufman Pattern Reasoning ($r = .43$) as the two subtests measured the same construct. A partial correlation was also observed between NEPSY Block Construction and Tactile Pattern Reasoning ($r = .21$) and Kaufman Pattern Reasoning ($r = .32$). Modest correlations were found between early literacy and both Tactile Pattern Reasoning ($r = .36$) and Kaufman Pattern Reasoning ($r = .37$).

Thus, although ZamCAT has not yet been used on a wide scale across cultures, it is relatively sensitive to the cultural context. Its cultural responsiveness is embedded not only in the systematic adaptation process but also in the utilization of locally available materials which are familiar to the child within the African context. Of great significance is that ZamCAT incorporates existing instruments, thus allowing comparison with standardized instruments. Because the instrument captures various domain areas, it offers potential for the assessment of school readiness as well as identification of children at potential risk for developmental problems. The test is currently being validated in Tanzania and Malawi.

Conclusions

The process of test development for children in Africa has received much less attention than it deserves, given the serious challenges posed by the prevailing practice of importing standardized tests from the Western world. The two case studies presented in this chapter represent preliminary steps toward filling the gap that exists in reliable, valid, and appropriately standardized instruments for the assessment of children for detection of developmental risk, differential diagnosis, individualized program planning, monitoring, evaluation, or research. Astatke and Serpell (2000) presented a process model for development and validation of a procedure for studying a construct in a new cultural setting. Ideally, they note, the first step should be a conceptual one, coordinating intuition, common sense, and knowledge about the world with existing theory and empirical literature on the one hand and local prevalence estimates on the other to generate a checklist of constructs whose relevance should then be appraised. Only when this conceptual work has been done should the researcher embark on operationalizing constructs and expanding their definition. In practice, however, test development in Africa has often been driven by narrowly focused research questions or by pressing practical needs. We hope that our account of two particular cases of test development in Zambia will serve to provoke constructive debate on how to pay attention to issues of measurement while concurrently conducting applied research and promoting enhanced services for young children and their families.

References

Abubakar, A., Van De Vijver, F. J. R., Mithwani, S., Obiero, E., Lewa, N., Kenga, S., … Holding, P. (2007). Assessing developmental outcomes in children from Kilifi, Kenya, following prophylaxis for seizures in cerebral malaria. *Journal of Health Psychology*, 12, 417–430.

Alant, E., Tesner, H., & Taljaardt, E. (1992). Narrative performance in context: Analysis and implications within a South African context. *Child Language Teaching and Therapy*, 8, 188–204.

Alcock, K. J., Holding, P. A., Mung'ala-Odera, V., & Newton, C. R. J. C. (2008). Constructing tests of cognitive abilities for schooled and unschooled children. *Journal of Cross-cultural Psychology*, 39, 529–551.

Ardila, A., & Roselli, M. (2003). Educational effects on the ROCF performance. In J. Knight & E. Kaplan (Eds.), *Rey-Osterrieth complex figure handbooks* (pp. 659–667). New York, NY: Psychological Assessment Resources.

Astatke, H., & Serpell, R. (2000). Testing the application of a Western scientific theory of AIDS risk behavior among adolescents in Ethiopia. *Journal of Pediatric Psychology*, 25(6), 367–379.

Dasen, P. R., Barthélémy, D., Kan, E., Kouamé, K., Daouda, K., Adjéi, K. K., & Assandé, N. (1985). N'Glouele, l'intelligence chez les Baoulé [N'Glouele, intelligence according to the Baoulé]. *Archives de psychologie*, 53, 293–324.

Denton, F. K., & McPhee, C. (2009). *The children born in 2001 at kindergarten entry: First findings from the kindergarten data collection of the early childhood longitudinal study—birth cohort (ECLS-B)* (NCES 2010-005). Washington, DC: U.S. Department of Education.

Deregowski, J. B. (1968). Difficulties in pictorial perception in Africa. *British Journal of Psychology*, 59, 195–204.

Deregowski, J. B. (1974). Teaching African children pictorial depth perception: In search of a method. *Perception*, 3(3), 309–312.

Deregowski, J. B., & Serpell, R. (1971). Performance on a sorting task: A cross cultural experiment. *International Journal of Psychology*, 6, 273–281.

Durkin, M. S., & Maenner, M. (2014). Screening for developmental disabilities in epidemiologic studies in low- and middle-income countries. In S. O. Okpaku (Ed.),

Essentials of global mental health (pp. 187–194). Cambridge, UK: Cambridge University Press.
Durojaiye, M. O. A. (1984). The impact of psychological testing on education and personal selection in Africa. International Journal of Psychology, 19, 135–144.
Ettling, D., Phiri, J. T., Msango, H., Matafwali, B., Mandyata, J. M., Mudaala-Simfukwe, E., ... Mwansa, A. B. (2006). Child development assessment in Zambia: A study of developmental norms of Zambian children aged 0–72 months. Lusaka, Zambia: Ministry of Education and UNICEF.
Ezeilo, B. (1978). Validating Panga Munthu Test and Porteus Maze Test (wooden form) in Zambia. International Journal of Psychology, 13, 333–342.
Fink, G., Matafwali, B., Moucheraud, C., & Zuilkowski, S. S. (2012). The Zambian Early Childhood Development Project—2010 Assessment Final Report. Retrieved from http://developingchild.harvard.edu/activities/global_initiative/zambian_project/
Frijda, N., & Jahoda, G. (1966). On the scope and methods of cross-cultural research. International Journal of Psychology, 1, 109–127.
Fryers, T. (1986). Screening for developmental disabilities in developing countries: Problems and perspectives. In K. Marfo, S. Walker, & B. Charles (Eds.), Childhood disability in developing countries (pp. 27–40). New York: Praeger.
Greenfield, P. M. (1997). You can't take it with you: Why ability assessments don't cross cultures. American Psychologist, 52, 1115–1124.
Grigorenko, E. L., Geissler, P. W., Prince, R., Okatcha, F., Nokes, C., Kenny, D. A., Bundy, D. A., & Sternberg, R. J. (2001). The organisation of Luo conceptions of intelligence: a study of implicit theories in a Kenyan village. International Journal of Behavioral Development, 25(4), 367–378.
Hambleton, R. (1994). Guidelines for adapting educational and psychological tests: A progress report. European Journal of Psychological Assessment, 10, 229–244.
Harkness, J. A., Van de Vijver, F. J. R., & Johnson, T. P. (2003). Questionnaire design in comparative research. In J. A. Harkness, F. J. R. Van de Vijver, & P. P. Mohler (Eds.), Cross-cultural survey methods (pp. 19–34). Hoboken, NJ: Wiley.
Harris, D. B. (1963). Children's drawings as measures of intellectual maturity: A revision and extension of the Goodenough Draw-a-Man test. New York, NY: Harcourt, Brace & World.
Herdman, M., Fox-Rushby, J., & Badia, X. (1998). A model of equivalence in the cultural adaptation of HRQoL instruments: The universality approach. Quality of Life Research, 7, 323–335.
Hilliard, A. G. (1975). The strengths and weaknesses of cognitive tests for young children. In J. D. Andrews (Ed.), One child indivisible (pp. 17–33). Washington, DC: National Association for the Education of Young Children.
Holding, P., Abubakar, A., & Kitsao-Wekulo, P. (2008). A systematic approach to test and questionnaire adaptation in an African context. Paper presented at 3 MC Conference. Retrieved from http://csdiworkshop.org/v2/index.php/118-2008-3mc-conference/2008-presentations/session-9
Hudson, W. (1962). Cultural problems in pictorial perception. South African Journal of Social Psychology, 52, 193–208.
Jukes, M. C. H., & Grigorenko, E. L. (2010). Assessment of cognitive abilities in multi-ethnic countries: The case of the Wolof and Mandinka in the Gambia. British Journal of Educational Psychology, 80, 77–97.
Kathuria, R., & Serpell, R. (1998). Standardisation of the Panga Munthu Test—A nonverbal Cognitive Test Developed in Zambia. Journal of Negro Education, 67, 228–241.
Kaufman, A. S., & Kaufman, N. L. (2004). Kaufman assessment battery for children (2nd ed.). Circle Pines, MN: American Guidance Service.
Korkman, M., Kirk, U., & Kemp, S. L. (2007). NEPSY II. Administrative manual. San Antonio, TX: Psychological Corporation.

Matafwali, B. (2005). *Nature and prevalence of reading difficulties in the third grade: Lusaka rural and urban schools* (MA dissertation). University of Zambia, Lusaka. Retrieved from http://dspace.unza.zm:8080/xmlui/handle/123456789/411

Mitchell, D. M., & Brown, R. I. (Eds.). (1991). *Early intervention studies for young children with special needs.* London, UK: Chapman & Hall.

Mpofu, E., & Nyanungo, K. R. L. (1998). Educational and psychological testing in Zimbabwean schools: Past, present and future. *European Journal of Psychological Assessment, 14,* 71–90.

Mshelua, A. Y., & Lapidus, L. B. (1990). Depth picture perception in relation to cognitive style and training in non-Western children. *Journal of Cross-Cultural Psychology, 21,* 414–433.

Mundy-Castle, A. C. (1966). Pictorial depth perception in Ghanaian children. *International Journal of Psychology, 1,* 169–172.

Mwaura, P. A. M., Sylva, K., & Malmberg, L.-E. (2008). Evaluating the Madrasa preschool programme in East Africa: A quasi-experimental study. *International Journal of Early Years Education, 16,* 237–255.

Nampijja, M., Apule, B., Lule, S., Akurut, H., Muhangi, L., Elliot, A. M., & Alcock, K. J. (2010). Adaptation of Western measures of cognition for assessing 5-year-old semi-urban Ugandan children. *British Journal of Educational Psychology, 80,* 15–30.

Nell, V. (2000). *Cross-cultural neuropsychological assessment: Theory and practice.* Mahwah, NJ: Lawrence Erlbaum.

Ngenda, I. (2011). *Construct validity of the Panga Munthu test: A cross-sectional study of early childhood years in Zambia (4–6 years)* (MA dissertation). University of Zambia, Lusaka. Retrieved from http://dspace.unza.zm:8080/xmlui/handle/123456789/1057

Okonji, O. M. (1971). The effects of familiarity on classification. *Journal of Cross-Cultural Psychology, 2,* 39–49.

Omari, I. M., & MacGinitie, W. H. (1974). Some pictorial artifacts in studies of African children's pictorial perception. *Child Development, 45,* 535–539.

Opolot, J. A. (1976). Differential cognitive cues in pictorial depth perception among Ugandan children. *International Journal of Psychology, 11,* 81–88.

Retschitzki, J. (1988). L'apprentissage des stratégies dans le jeu d'awélé. In R. Bureau & D. Saivre (Eds.), *Apprentissage et cultures, les manières d'apprendre* (pp. 213–229). Paris, France: Éditions Karthala.

Rogoff, B. (1981). Schooling and the development of cognitive skills. In H. C. Triandis & A. Heron (Eds.), *Handbook of cross-cultural psychology* (Vol. 4, pp. 233–294). Rockleigh, NJ: Allyn & Bacon.

Schuurman, M. M. (1995). Opportunities and constraints for research on education and human development in Africa: Focus on assessment and special education. *Comparative Education Review, 37,* 181–222.

Serpell, R. (1971). Preference for specific orientation of abstract shapes among Zambian children. *Journal of Cross-Cultural Psychology, 2,* 225–239.

Serpell, R. (1974). *Estimates of intelligence in a rural community of eastern Zambia* (Human Development Research Unit Reports, 25, 78 pp.). Lusaka, Zambia: University of Zambia (limited circulation [mimeo]).

Serpell, R. (1977). Estimates of intelligence in a rural community of eastern Zambia. In F. M. Okatcha (Ed.), *Modern psychology and cultural adaptation* (pp. 179–216). Nairobi, Kenya: Swahili Language Consultants and Publishers.

Serpell, R. (1979). How specific are perceptual skills? A cross of pattern reproduction. *British Journal of Psychology, 70,* 365–380.

Serpell, R. (1988). Childhood disability in sociocultural context: Assessment and information needs for effective services. In P. R. Dasen, J. W. Berry, & N. Sartorius (Eds.), *Health and crosscultural psychology: Towards applications* (pp. 256–280). Newbury Park, CA: Sage.

Serpell, R. (1990) Audience, culture and psychological explanation: A reformulation of the emic-etic problem in cross-cultural psychology. *Quarterly Newsletter of the Laboratory of Comparative Human Cognition, 12*(3), 99–132. Retrieved from http://lchc.ucsd.edu/Histarch/newsletters.html

Serpell, R. (1993). *The significance of schooling. Life journeys in an African society.* Cambridge: Cambridge University Press.

Serpell, R. (1999). Opportunities and constraints for research on education and human development in Africa: Focus on assessment and special education. *Prospects, 29*(3), 349–363.

Serpell, R. (2000). Intelligence and culture. In R. J. Sternberg (Ed.), *The handbook of intelligence* (pp. 549–577). Cambridge, UK & New York, NY: Cambridge University Press.

Serpell, R., & Hatano, G. (1997). Education, schooling, and literacy. In J. W. Berry, P. R. Dasen, & T. S. Sarawathi (Eds.), *Handbook of cross-cultural psychology. Vol. 2: Basic processes and human development* (pp. 339–376). Boston, MA: Allyn & Bacon.

Serpell, R., & Haynes, B. (2004). The cultural practice of intelligence testing: Problems of international export. In R. J. Sternberg & E. Grigorenko (Eds.), *Culture and competence: Contexts of life success* (pp. 163–185). Washington, DC: American Psychological Association.

Serpell, R., & Jere-Folotiya, J. (2008). Developmental assessment, cultural context, gender and schooling in Zambia. *International Journal of Psychology, 43*, 88–96.

Serpell, R., & Jere-Folotiya, J. (2011). Basic education for children with special needs in Zambia: Progress and challenges in the translation of policy into practice. *Psychology and Developing Societies, 23*, 211–245.

Stemler, S. E., Chamvu, F., Chart, H., Jarvin, L., Jere, J., Hart, L., … Grigorenko, E. L. (2009). Assessing competencies in reading and mathematics in Zambian children. In E. L. Grigorenko (Ed.), *Multicultural psychoeducational assessment* (pp. 166–206). New York, NY: Springer.

Sternberg, R. J., Conway, B., Ketron, J., & Bernstein, M. (1981). People's conceptions of intelligence. *Journal of Personality and Social Psychology, 4*, 37–55.

Super, C., & Harkness, S. (1986). The developmental niche: A conceptualization at the interface of child and culture. *International Journal of Behavioral Development, 9*, 545–569.

Sylva, K., Melhuish, E., Sammons, P., Siraj-Blatchford, I., & Taggart, B. (2011). Preschool quality and educational outcomes at age 11: Low quality has little benefit. *Journal of Early Childhood Research, 9*(2), 109–124.

Van de Vijver, F. J. R. (2002). Cross-cultural assessment: Value for money? *Applied Psychology: An International Review, 51*, 545–566.

Van de Vijver, F. J. R., & Poortinga, Y. H. (1997). Towards an integrated analysis of bias in cross-cultural assessment. *European Journal of Psychological Assessment, 13*, 29–37.

Van de Vijver, F. J. R., & Tanzer, N. K. (1997/2004). Bias and equivalence in cross-cultural assessment: An overview. *European Review of Applied Psychology, 47*, 263–279. (republished in volume 54 (2004) 119–135)

Vernon, P. E. (1969). *Intelligence and cultural environment.* London, UK: Methuen.

Wicherts, J. M., Dolan, C. V., Carlson, J. S., & van der Maas, H. L. N. (2010). Raven's test performance of Sub-Saharan Africans: Average performance, psychometric properties, and the Flynn effect. *Learning and Individual Differences, 20*(3), 135–151.

Wober, M. (1974). Towards an understanding of the Kiganda concept of intelligence. In J. W. Berry & P. R. Dasen (Eds.), *Culture and cognition: Readings in cross-cultural psychology* (pp. 261–280). London, UK: Methuen.

Zigler, E., & Finn-Stevenson, M. (1992). Applied developmental psychology. In M. C. Bornstein & M. E. Lamb (Eds.), *Developmental psychology: An advanced textbook* (3rd ed., pp. 677–729). Hillsdale, NJ: Erlbaum.

Zuilkowski, S. S., Fink, G., & Matafwali, B. (2011, April). *Assessing child development in Zambia: The ZAMCAT project.* Paper presented at Biennial Conference of the Society for Research in Child Development (SRCD), Montreal, Canada.

Zuilkowski, S. S., Fink, G., Moucheraud, C., & Matafwali, B. (2012). Early childhood education, child development and school readiness: Evidence from Zambia. *South African Journal of Childhood Education,* 2(2), 117–136.

BEATRICE MATAFWALI *is a lecturer and head of the Department of Educational Psychology, Sociology, and Special Education in the School of Education, University of Zambia.*

ROBERT SERPELL *is a professor of applied developmental psychology and coordinator of the Center for Promotion of Literacy in Sub-Saharan Africa (CAPOLSA) in the School of Humanities and Social Sciences, University of Zambia.*

Serpell, R., & Marfo, K. (2014). Some growth points in African child development research. In R. Serpell & K. Marfo (Eds.), *Child development in Africa: Views from inside. New Directions for Child and Adolescent Development, 146,* 97–112.

6

Some Growth Points in African Child Development Research

Robert Serpell, Kofi Marfo

Abstract

We reflect on ways in which research presented in earlier chapters responds to challenges of generating an African child development field and identify additional issues calling for the field's attention. The chapters collectively display a variety of African contexts and reflexive evidence of the authors' African cultural roots. Connecting research with African audiences demands cooperative communication between educational practitioners and parents with low literacy, and cross-sector communication among professionals. Intracultural exploration of factors influencing the pattern of human development has begun to document the potential of indigenous African cultures as a fund of resources for enhancing child development. Priority topics for future African developmental research include multilingualism, musical performance, socially distributed caregiving, and the relation between adolescence and economic activity. Integration of multiple disciplines in the application of research-based principles to service delivery in the fields of community-based (re)habilitation and early childhood care and education calls for researcher collaboration with practitioners. © 2014 Wiley Periodicals, Inc.

Key features of the African child development field envisioned by Marfo (2011) are that it should (a) address issues that are important within Africa's own context, particularly those dimensions of development, conceptions of development, and practices around development that are intrinsically African; (b) contribute to and benefit from conceptions and knowledge of children in other societies; (c) be pluralistic in terms of research paradigms and methodologies, and seek to integrate multiple disciplines; (d) recognize sociocultural diversity both across the continent and within nations; and (e) be a living, real-world field informed by a symbiotic relationship between academic researchers and professional practitioners in the community. In this chapter, we reflect on the degree to which Chapters 2–5 in this volume resonate with that vision.

Responding to the Challenges of Generating an African Child Development Field

First, we consider how successfully they respond collectively to the challenges we posed in Chapter 1: (a) the challenge of African reflexivity; (b) the challenge of contextual diversity, relevance, and practical importance; and (c) the challenge of intelligibility to local audiences.

The Challenge of African Reflexivity. In addition to personal experience growing up as a child in an African society, each of the authors has been engaged firsthand with African children and families as a researcher, with an African society as a citizen, and with an African community of knowledge as a student, a teacher, and a writer. Moreover, each has traveled from their home base in Kenya, Zimbabwe, or Zambia to many other countries on the continent, sharing ideas with other African scholars. And they have spent time in analytical discussion with scholars based in many other parts of the world, comparing and contrasting the range of situations in which African children develop with those prevailing in other regions.

In their contributions to this volume each author identifies a number of ways in which the African context of child development is distinctive, as well as acknowledging the relevance of a number of theories developed by scholars in the so-called mainstream of the academy for understanding African child development. They also share a particular interest in the period of early childhood from birth until the age of about 8.

The Challenge of Contextual Diversity, Relevance, and Practical Importance. These authors' studies sampled a variety of ethnic and linguistic groups, as well as both rural and urban ecological settings, with perhaps a bias toward the rural areas where the vast majority of Africa's children are growing up. Grounding their research in questions and concerns that emanate specifically from the conditions of African children developing and learning in the context of families, communities, and schools, the authors demonstrate responsiveness to the criteria of contextual relevance and practical importance in African developmental science.

The Challenge of Intelligibility to African Audiences. All of the authors are deeply engaged with this issue. As Ng'asike puts it, in Kenya "educationally disadvantaged pastoralist communities like the Turkana find it hard to engage with a system of education that is impossible to comprehend" (p. 47). Yet it is precisely such communities to whose interests current efforts all over the continent to increase access to education are addressed. Like the pioneers of Head Start in the context of America's War on Poverty in the 1960s, governments, missions, and NGOs in Africa are inspired by the advocacy of UNICEF, the World Bank, and other international organizations to believe that increasing access to Early Chilhood Development Care and Educational provision will prevent the loss of potential by protecting children against insidious risks arising from the poverty of their home environments (Engle et al., 2007).

Cooperative Communication Between Educational Practitioners and Parents With Low Literacy. Ironically, as Ng'asike points out in Chapter 3, "ECD children continue to learn at the doorstep of their own cultures in English from curriculum content based on Western ideology to the extent that the knowledge of families in the villages is ignored by the oppressive education system" (p. 48). In Chapter 4, Ngwaru also affirms that rural African communities contain abundant sociocultural "funds of knowledge that remained untapped" (p. 71) by current ECD programs in Zimbabwe and Tanzania.

These insights from Ng'asike and Ngwaru have important curricular and pedagogical ramifications. Marfo and Biersteker (2011) advanced the perspective that pedagogy, by virtue of entailing not just the act of teaching but also the connections that exist among teaching, culture, organization, and mechanisms of social control, "is by definition context-bound and value-laden" (p. 81). Consequently, it is axiomatic that the starting points for curriculum design and instructional practice in the African context will be knowledge and understandings about the local ecology of development. Within that ecosystem, child development research will need to explore the modalities and pathways to learning that are evident in the ways that African children engage, and are socialized to engage, their object and social worlds.

Ng'asike presents an elaborate description in Chapter 3 of many of the elements of this knowledge base that are consistent with insights from the work of other African scholars (e.g., Marfo & Biersteker, 2011; Okwany, Ngutuku, & Muhangi, 2011). Based on their review of the literature on play in African contexts, Marfo and Biersteker identified pedagogical insights and principles that they deemed compatible with Euro-American conceptions of constructivist and discovery learning. Adapting the principles of constructivist instruction to mobilize the potential of experiential domains and sociocultural practices that are familiar to children in their locality should give rise to optimal pathways for their cognitive development. A critical task that will flow from such research is the design and activation of ways to systematically reorient curriculum design away from the *status quo*. In the words of Marfo and Biersteker (2011), "it is not sufficient to merely include local games, songs, and activities, and play materials in the existing curriculum" (p. 81). Integrating indigenous cultural resources into the design and delivery of services to young children and their families will require policy changes and investments in research on curriculum design and evaluation.

In Ngwaru's view, responsibility for this missed opportunity lies not only with curriculum developers and teachers, but also with parents. Like many others working in the field of programmatic promotion of ECD, he emphasizes the role of parents in supporting the education of children beyond their own level of certified academic achievement. His research reveals some intriguing points of convergence in teachers' and parents' ethnotheories about literacy "socialization." He points to the consistency between, on the one hand, parents' inclination to see themselves as not being knowledgeable enough to be helpful to their children's literacy development, and, on the other hand, teachers' general tendency to perceive parents as lacking the knowledge and expertise to contribute meaningfully to their children's development of literacy skills.

A similar interpretation was advanced by Serpell (1993) of the failure of Parent Teacher Associations at rural Zambian schools in the 1980s to generate a constructive form of cooperative communication between parents and professionals about the school's substantive educational agenda:

> parents conspire with teachers to perpetuate their own exclusion from the kind of discourse which would be most productive, by insisting on only discussing school success in terms of its external facets as a mode of access to secondary school, which in turn is construed instrumentally as a route for obtaining credentials to deploy in the formal sector labour-market. (p. 141)

Both groups fail to recognize, let alone capitalize on, the culturally embedded *funds of knowledge* that are increasingly being identified by scholars as critical assets in any effort to (a) enhance learning by infusing locally compatible learning modes into instruction and (b) make learning meaningful by expanding curricular content to include content with local relevance.

Ngwaru hinges his intervention recommendations around empowering parents to understand and exert their role in their children's education. Equally important would be to empower teachers to move beyond the orthodoxy of Western-style curricula content and pedagogy. While both parents and teachers have been socialized into discounting the significance of content and processes within their own culture for children's literacy learning, teachers bear the additional burden of having received professional education that accorded no significance to local knowledge or to culturally primed developmental inputs. A valuable focus of applied (or action-) research would be to develop a program of professional development to reorient teachers toward cultural affirmation, paving the way for meaningful integration of local and exogenous knowledge and practices.

Interdisciplinary and Cross-Sector Communication Among Professionals. Abubakar points out in Chapter 2 that "many studies on the impact of HIV infection on children have focused on the potential contribution of biomedical mediators (e.g., disease staging) while ignoring psychosocial issues. On the other hand, the literature on psychosocial risk has been strongly influenced by studies on HIV-affected children. There is a need for more work looking at these areas concurrently" (p. 34). As she demonstrates, the interdependence of biomedical and psychosocial factors is extremely complex and will not be understood well enough to allow for effective, evidence-based intervention unless African researchers with varied disciplinary backgrounds and expertise put their heads together to educate one another and build truly interdisciplinary programs of applied research and development.

Even within the field of psychology, different specialized branches often tend to ignore one another's advances. Professionals and policymakers in the health or education sector often turn for technical advice to a particular type of specialist, grounded more in customary patterns of interaction or institutionalized channels. Medical practitioners are more likely to learn from colleagues in psychiatry, neuropsychology, or pediatrics, while teachers and curriculum developers are more exposed to educational psychology, psycholinguistics, and psychometrics. The perspectives of cultural, cross-cultural, and developmental psychology are not well represented in the basic professional curricula or indeed the specialized professional journals attached to the training and orientation of teachers, doctors, or nurses. Interdisciplinary communication, let alone cooperation, is more likely to emerge in institutional settings with titles such as *community health* or *human development*.

Even when the planners and administrators of an intervention program recognize the need for a specialized activity such as the assessment of children's development, it is quite likely that reliance on a traditional pattern of consultancy will result in access only to a narrow range of evidence, unless scholars make an effort to reach out to communicate with a variety of audiences. In the absence of such bridge-building, it is likely that the problematic practice of "importing standardized tests from the Western world" (p. 91) criticized by Matafwali and Serpell in Chapter 5 will persist. The challenge, as they put it, is for applied researchers to articulate feasible and effective ways "to pay attention to issues of measurement while concurrently conducting applied research and promoting enhanced services for young children and their families" (p. 92).

Lessons Learned

Collectively these chapters illustrate the complexity of the issues facing research on child development in Africa and the diversity of perspectives adopted by contemporary indigenous scholars on research strategies for investigating them. Underlying that diversity, however, all of the contributors to this volume seem to share a sense that intracultural exploration of regional, national, and intranational group factors influencing the pattern of human development is a more productive focus for their research than cross-cultural comparisons of human behavior using cultural groups as an independent variable. Comparison with Western society is an implicit source of interpretation for many of their findings, but the emphasis of their conclusions is firmly intracultural. This shift of focus is reminiscent of the emergence of cultural psychology in the 1980s (discussed in Chapter 1), partly inspired by and partly reacting against the directly comparative focus of cross-cultural psychology.

As Abubakar put it eloquently in her proposal for an invited symposium at the 21st international conference of the IACCP, held in 2012 (for the first time in Africa) at the University of Stellenbosch in South Africa:

> Africa and other regions of the Majority World have been the incubator of much (cross-) cultural research in psychology. However, the data and knowledge gained often have been export products rather than building blocks for individual and national development. Academic reasons for the limited relevance of cross-cultural knowledge discussed in the literature include:
>
> - Adversarial debates about the scope, or lack of it, for transfer of psychological principles and knowledge across cultures (universalism versus relativism debate).
> - A western focus in the major topics addressed by researchers in cross-cultural research and the need for indigenous psychologies to address local issues.
> - The search for explanations of the current state of affairs in the psychological make-up of the members of a society rather than in the circumstances they live in (culture as external versus culture as internal).
>
> In this symposium participants will explore how such issues that have become part of the heritage of the field can be left behind. They will outline their vision on how research on behaviour and culture can be made more relevant for the more than 5 milliard clients whose interests so far have been underrepresented.

Another area of consensus among several of the contributors to the present volume is the value of indigenous culture as a fund of resources for enhancing the development of children. Ng'asike's chapter is the most explicit in its endorsement of this focus of research. Ngwaru also highlights it as one of the premises of the challenge he identifies of mobilizing parent engagement with ECE. This complementarity between the research directions articulated by Ngwaru and Ng'asike has notable implications for the development of curriculum policy and classroom pedagogy.

Addressing Dimensions that are Intrinsically African. In an earlier period of the African academy, Wober (1975) criticized African scholars for being too ready to equate appropriation of Western culture as a guarantee of social progress through psychological modernization. But one of the most impressive African scholars of that generation, Michael Ogbolu Okonji, drew generative inspiration from both Piaget and Witkin. He enriched the global database with observations of African child development collected with their methods, and interpreted through their explanatory frameworks, as well as extending both theories with new insights. He challenged the universality of Piaget's methods by showing how the level of a child's intellectual development reflected in classificatory behavior depended on the child's familiarity with the materials to be classified (Okonji, 1971). And he challenged many aspects of Witkin's theory in the light of inconsistencies when the tests were applied in African and other non-Western cultural contexts (Okonji, 1980). Likewise, the current generation of African scholars has found utility for products of the Western scientific tradition in their studies of African child development: Abubakar's neuropsychology, Matafwali's psychometrics, and Ngwaru's membership of the ECD community all represent links to the "mainstream" of contemporary science and professional practice.

Perhaps of greater significance is the recognition by several of these Africanist scholars that within the broad compass of Western scholarship some strands of research are explicitly preoccupied with challenging the mainstream. Both Ngwaru and Ng'asike draw attention to the theoretical fruitfulness of the neo-Vygotskian "funds of knowledge" perspective advanced by Moll and his colleagues in their research and interventions among Hispanic sections of the U.S. population (Moll & Greenberg, 1990). They also acknowledge that Western scholars conducting child development research in Africa and elsewhere (such as Moll, Amanti, Neff & Gonzalez, 1992; Rogoff, 2003; Super & Harkness, 2002) have generated useful theoretical constructs for interpreting child development in its local cultural context.

Yet these scholars also display a growing recognition that while these constructs, theories, and programs do throw valuable light on certain aspects of contemporary conditions in Africa, they also tend to marginalize, and in some cases distort, the interpretation of constructs embedded in those cultural systems of meaning that have not been part of the scientific discourse giving rise to mainstream Western theories of social science. Ng'asike confronts this issue head on in Chapter 3 by pointing out the anomaly of imposing alien texts and instructional routines on children whose home communities are rich with stories, practices, and learning opportunities, all in the name of cognitive enrichment. His critique of this flawed approach to curriculum and instruction in Kenya's ECE programs draws on a reconceptualist philosophy that is at once both Western in its immediate genesis and highly critical of Western cultural hegemony (cf. Kessler & Swadener, 1992).

Another example of the value of foregrounding local realities for innovative analysis is the topic of multilingualism. Until the 1970s, multilingualism was most often characterized by researchers in the African region as a challenging social consequence of imperialism. Currently, it is widely acknowledged as a manifestation of cognitive power to be actively promoted as a resource for building metacognitive flexibility and social harmony (Banda, 2009; Prah & Brock-Utne, 2009).

Closely related to the agenda of documenting the cognitive and social potential of multilingualism is the exploration of which dimensions of the indigenous African languages are most helpful to analyze and promote. Topics such as dialectal variation and orthography have attracted greater attention from the discipline of linguistics than from psychology. The implications of developmental psycholinguistics for the design of interventions to promote initial literacy, a key dimension of education, are receiving growing appreciation among policymakers, at least in Zambia. The Centre for Promotion of Literacy in Sub-Saharan Africa (CAPOLSA, 2014) at the University of Zambia grew out of a research partnership with a Western psychology research team at the University of Jyvaskyla in Finland (Jere-Folotiya et al., 2014). Yet its expanded agenda (Serpell, 2014) includes promotion of writing and publication of child-friendly literature in several of the indigenous African languages, both as a pragmatic way of increasing the national stock of resources for initial readers to exercise their skills and at a broader level to enhance the public legitimacy of indigenous cultural resources—an example perhaps of what some African political thinkers have hailed as an African Renaissance.

Other emerging research themes with the potential to foreground phenomena of distinctive importance in African childhood include musical performance, socially distributed caregiving, and the relation between adolescence and economic activity. A fruitful collaboration between the disciplines of music, anthropology, and psychology has begun to focus on musical performance as not only a domain of entertainment, but also a cultural resource for both cognitive and socioemotional development because of its widely acknowledged role in celebrating social harmony (Mtonga, 2012; Mukela, 2013; Ng'andu & Herbst, 2004; Nyota & Mapara, 2008). This theoretical perspective harks back to an earlier theme of African scholarship that celebrated the extraordinary cultural wealth of African music and its productive influence on the music of the United States (Gridley & Rave, 1984; Lipsitz, 1994; Nketia, 1963, 1973).

The concept of socially distributed caregiving (Weisner, 1997) has begun to give theoretical legitimacy to a shift away from earlier Western views of the practice, widespread in Africa, of delegating the care of young children to preadolescent youth as a dereliction of maternal duty or as a distraction from the official agenda of schooling. Instead, various African scholars have acknowledged the practice as a strategic sociocultural practice with unique affordances for socioemotional and moral development (Nsamenang, 2012; Serpell, 2008; Serpell, Mumba, & Chansa-Kabali, 2011). This insight has also connected with applied research promoting the mobilization of children as agents of health education through the child-to-child approach (Hawes, 1988; Morley & Woodland, 1988; Mumba, 2000).

A recent volume containing several studies of the connection between participation in economically productive activities and the kind of knowledge, skills, and attitudes acquired by children growing up in Southwestern Ethiopia is introduced by Abebe and Kjorholt (2013) with the following rationale:

> ideals and assumptions about childhood and what it means to be a child that are anchored in the global north are not helpful analytically (i.e. to understand the lives of Ethiopian children) and from a policy point of view (to improve their well-being). ...Local knowledge about the varieties of childhood and of children about material social practices helps both to complete the picture and contextualize what it takes to come of age in contemporary Ethiopian society. (p. 34)

Cross-Sector Integration of Multidimensional Service Delivery to Children and Youth. The importance of integrating theoretical insights from multiple disciplines for the understanding of child development is reflected in the design of two currently salient applications of research in Africa: responses to the HIV and AIDS pandemic, and interventions to support early childhood development.

HIV and AIDS. The reality of multiple risk conditions underscored by Abubakar in her account of research on children affected by HIV and AIDS (Chapter 2) has important implications for professional service delivery, which are already receiving attention in the highly active community of service providers responding to the pandemic. To understand the impact of the pandemic on child development, we need to think beyond the impact of infection on the central nervous system, and include indirect influences mediated by economic adversity arising from the prolonged illness and premature death of primary caregivers, as well as socially mediated constraints arising from the stigma surrounding the disease (Bond, 2006). Increasingly, researchers on preventive health education are seeking ways not only to change the knowledge and practices of sexually active youth to protect them against infection (Bhana & Petersen, 2009), but also ways to reduce prejudice and promote social support among the uninfected population (e.g., Campbell, Nair, Maimane, & Nicholson, 2007), to build community and outreach service support for home-based care (cf. Ogden, Esim, & Grown, 2006), and to promote self-advocacy among persons living with AIDS (e.g., Henderson, 2006). It is becoming clear that the challenges of service programming for orphans and vulnerable children call for close attention to the attitudes and needs of elderly members of African rural communities who carry a large proportion of the burden of care (Oburu & Palmerus, 2003), and to the dynamics of sociocultural change in patterns of distributed responsibility for child care and socialization (Weisner, 1997). While some surveys have concluded that Africa's renowned extended family system may be collapsing under the excessive pressure of a dramatic increase in the number of orphans (Monasch & Boerma, 2004), a more productive focus of research is to explore its potential resilience and adaptability to the challenges of the pandemic (Abebe & Aase, 2007; Kilbride & Kilbride, 1997; Oburu, 2009; Oleke, Blystad, Rekdal, & Moland, 2007).

The sociocultural focus of programmatic intervention in response to the HIV and AIDS pandemic resonates with an earlier field of applied research and intervention on community-based (re)habilitation (CBR) of children with disabilities (Nabuzoka, 1986, 1989; Serpell, 1986). Several practitioners in Africa and other Majority World settings began in that period to explore ways of delivering education and developmental interventions to children with special needs in their homes (e.g., Marfo, 1983; Marfo, Walker, & Charles, 1983; McConkey, 1994; McConkey, Mariga, Braadland, & Mphole, 2000; Serpell, Mariga, & Harvey, 1993; Sturmey et al., 1992).

The principle of grounding services to children with serious disabilities within their family and local community was actively promoted by the World Health Organisation in the 1980s (WHO, 1983), invoking at least two complementary lines of justification, one economic and political and the other psychological and sociological.

> Affordable, immediate coverage of the majority of needy children and their families was a major theme in some of the WHO's early advocacy of CBR. But other, perhaps more significant, advantages can also be claimed for it relative to typical institutionally based service provision (Serpell, 1986). These include:
>
> - acknowledging and fostering family commitment to the welfare of a disabled child,
> - cultivating the growth of parental confidence in meeting the child's needs,
> - focusing on the child as a whole person,
> - recruitment of community involvement in the process of (re)habilitation, and
> - ensuring continuity of care over the lifetime of the individual. (Serpell & Jere-Folotiya, 2011, pp. 217–219)

Implementing these principles in practice calls for both theoretical articulation and empirical research, to ensure that they are not abusively co-opted for rhetorical purposes (cf. Rose, 2003), but give rise to genuine improvements in the lives of children and families who face daunting challenges to their survival and well-being.

Early Childhood Care, Development, and Education. A worldwide movement in public policy has gained momentum in the early 21st century to prioritize investment in young children as a global strategy. Building on the international movements for Children's Rights (UN General Assembly, 1989) and Education for All (United Nations Educational, Scientific, and Cultural Organization [UNESCO], 1990), advocates of early childhood development, care, and education (ECDCE) have made a case for priority attention to the provision of early childhood services. The influential International Child Development Steering Group (ICDSG) has argued that the ethics of social justice in response to economic inequalities and the logistical advantages of prevention over cure converge to mandate that priority should be given to early intervention to correct widespread conditions that place vast numbers of children in the first few years of life at risk of premature death, developmental disability, or pathology (Engle et al., 2007; Grantham-McGregor et al., 2007; Walker et al., 2007). While their invocation of statistical evidence has helped to give momentum to a valuable international movement for progressive social change, the approach of the ICDSG "tends to exaggerate the degree of consensus within the scientific community in order to convince lay audiences and funding agencies that science has come up with a definitive solution" (Serpell & Nsamenang, 2014, p. 12). Inspired by the success of UNICEF's strategic focus in the 1980s on promotion of Growth-monitoring, Oral rehydration therapy, Breast-feeding, and Immunization (GOBI), "a new orthodoxy seems to be emerging, designed to enhance the development of children's cognitive and social–emotional competence through stimulation and caregiver sensitivity. But psychosocial intervention to optimise the development of young children cannot be operationalized with the same degree of cross-cultural equivalence as a vaccine or breast-feeding" (Serpell & Nsamenang, 2014, p. 13).

Introducing the World Bank's landmark collection of studies, entitled *Africa's Future, Africa's Challenge: Early Childhood Care and Development in Sub-Saharan Africa*, the editors emphasized that the book "does not speak with one voice. It is polyphonic, as is Sub-Saharan Africa" (Pence, Evans & Garcia, 2008, p. 6). Indeed, "while a growing body of research is available about young children and their families from other parts of the world, particularly from the United States and Europe, there is a paucity of such information available within and about Africa" (Pence et al., 2008, p. 4). A programmatic overview of what can be learned from the limited research available was compiled by Marfo and Pence (2011) in a special section of the journal *Child Development Perspectives*. Reflecting on the implications for future research of the papers included in that publication and the larger set from which they were selected, the lead article on "strengthening Africa's contributions to child development research" underscored the imperative that globalization presents for increased applied developmental research in non-Western societies:

> Our children's lives are now lived at the intersection of local realities and inevitable forces of global change. Many children are being thrust into multiple worlds, in none of which they feel at home. How do formal and informal socialization agents prepare children with the competencies necessary to function optimally across contexts? Child development research has an important role to play by forging a better understanding of the competencies, attitudes, and emotional resources children need and use to navigate within and across different environments. (Marfo, Pence, LeVine, & LeVine, 2011, p. 108)

To address such questions validly and comprehensively, Marfo et al. (2011) advocate drawing "relevant perspectives and methods from the broad range of disciplines concerned with children's development— anthropology, the cognitive and neurosciences, developmental and behavioral pediatrics, education, nutritional science, psychology, public/ population health, sociology, etc." (p. 108).

In addition to the challenge of integrating or at least respectfully acknowledging the intellectual perspectives of those diverse academic traditions, we emphasize that in the current African context research should seek to build reciprocally beneficial linkages between basic and operational types of inquiry. Almost all contemporary African societies already acknowledge as a focus of service provision the importance of responding to the needs of children impacted by the HIV and AIDS pandemic, of children with disabilities, and of children aged between birth and entry into formal schooling. Practitioners who specialize in the delivery of such services require training in the application of professional practices. It is widely accepted that such practices should, whenever possible, be grounded in evidence. Collecting and publishing such evidence demand that researchers engage not only with policymakers, but also with serving professional practitioners, to understand the constraints under which they work and to share with them ways of addressing the practical challenges that demand their day-to-day attention. In addition to the medical field's "gold standard" of randomized control trials and theoretically driven projects that cast providers as implementers of action plans designed by researchers, productive alternative approaches include participatory action research designs, case studies, and autoethnographies. As Yoshikawa, Weisner, Kalil, and Way (2008) have explained, complementary strengths of qualitative and quantitative methods can often be productively mobilized within a single, mixed-methods design. By negotiating agreement on how to address theoretical and practical questions, researchers, policymakers, and practitioners will be better placed to generate reliable new knowledge about child development in Africa and mobilize that knowledge for the benefit of Africa's children.

References

Abebe, T., & Aase, A. (2007). Children, AIDS and the politics of orphan care in Ethiopia: The extended family revisited. *Social Science and Medicine, 64,* 2058–2069.

Abebe, T., & Kjorholt, A. T. (2013). Children, intergenerational relationships and local knowledge in Ethiopia. In T. Abebe & A. T. Kjorholt (Eds.), *Childhood and local knowledge in Ethiopia: Livelihoods, rights and intergenerational relationships* (pp. 9–42). Trondheim, Norway: Akademika Publishing.

Abubakar, A. (2012). Applied (cross-)cultural psychology for the Majority World. Invitation to contribute to a symposium at *21st International Conference of the IACCP*. University of Stellenbosch, South Africa (one page, limited circulation document).

Banda, F. (2009). Critical perspectives on language planning and policy in Africa: Accounting for the notion of multilingualism. *Stellenbosch Papers in Linguistics, 38,* 1–11.

Bhana, A., & Petersen, I. (2009). HIV and youth: A behavioural perspective. In P. Rohleder, L. Swartz, S. C. Kalichman, & L. C. Simbayi (Eds.), *HIV/AIDS in South Africa 25 years on* (pp. 55–68). New York, NY: Springer.

Bond, V. (2006). Stigma when there is no other option: Understanding how poverty fuels discrimination toward people living with HIV in Zambia. In S. Gillespie (Ed.), *AIDS, poverty, and hunger: Challenges and responses* (pp. 181–198). Washington, DC: International Food Policy Research Institute.

Campbell, C., Nair, Y., Maimane, S., & Nicholson, J. (2007). "Dying twice": A multilevel model of the roots of AIDS stigma in two South African communities. *Journal of Health Psychology, 12,* 403–416.

Centre for Promotion of Literacy in Sub-Saharan Africa, University of Zambia (CAPOLSA). (2014). Retrieved from School of Humanities & Social Sciences website: www.unza.zm

Engle, P. L., Black, M. M., Behrman, J. R., Cabral de Mello, M., Gertler, P. J., Kapiriri, L., … Young, M. E. (2007). Strategies to avoid the loss of developmental potential in more than 200 million children in the developing world. *Lancet, 369,* 229–242.

Grantham-McGregor, S., Cheung, Y. B., Cueto, S., Glewwe, P., Richter, L., & Strupp, B. (2007). International child development steering group. Developmental potential in the first 5 years for children in developing countries. *Lancet, 369,* 60–70.

Gridley, M. C., & Rave, W. (1984). Towards identification of African traits in early jazz. *The Black Perspective in Music, 12,* 44–56.

Hawes, H. (1988). *Child-to-child: Another path to learning*. Hamburg, Germany: UNESCO Institute for Education.

Henderson, P. C. (2006). South African AIDS orphans: Examining assumptions around vulnerability from the perspective of rural children and youth. *Childhood, 13,* 303–327.

Jere-Folotiya, J., Chansa-Kabali, T., Munachaka, J. C., Sampa, F., Yalukanda, C., Westerholm, J., … Lyytinen, H. (2014). The effect of using a mobile literacy game to improve literacy levels of grade one students in Zambian schools. *Educational Technology Research and Development, 62,* 417–432.

Kessler, S., & Swadener, B. B. (Eds.). (1992). *Reconceptualizing the early childhood curriculum: Beginning the dialogue*. New York, NY: Teachers College Press.

Kilbride, P. L., & Kilbride, J. C. (1997). Stigma, role overload, and delocalization among contemporary Kenyan women. In T. Weisner, C. Bradley, & P. L. Kilbride (Eds.),

African families and the crisis of social change (pp. 208–223). Westport, CT: Bergin & Garvey.

Lipsitz, G. (1994). *Dangerous crossroads: Popular music, post-modernism and the poetics of place*. London, UK: Verso.

Marfo, K. (1983). *Community-based approaches to disability prevention and early habilitation in the context of developing countries* (Occasional papers of the Center for International Education and Development, No. 2). Edmonton, Canada: Faculty of Education, University of Alberta.

Marfo, K. (2011). Envisioning an African child development field. *Child Development Perspectives, 5,* 140–147.

Marfo, K., & Biersteker, L. (2011). Exploring culture, play and early childhood education practice in African contexts. In S. Rogers (Ed.), *Rethinking play and pedagogy in early childhood education* (pp. 73–85). New York, NY: Routledge.

Marfo, K., & Pence, A. (2011). Special section on: Strengthening Africa's contributions to child development research. *Child Development Perspectives, 5*(2), 104–147.

Marfo, K., Pence, A. R., LeVine, R. A., & LeVine, S. (2011). Strengthening Africa's contributions to child development research: Introduction. *Child Development Perspectives, 5*(2), 104–111.

Marfo, K., Walker, S., & Charles, B. (1983). *Education and rehabilitation of the disabled in Africa—Vol. 1: Toward improved services*. Edmonton, Canada: University of Alberta, Center for International Education and Development.

McConkey, R. (1994). Using video as a teaching aid (in Zimbabwe). In M. J. Thorburn & K. Marfo (Eds.), *Practical approaches to childhood disability in developing countries: Insights from experience and research* (pp. 141–159). Tampa, FL: Global Age Publishing.

McConkey, R., Mariga, L., Braadland, N., & Mphole, P. (2000). Parents as trainers about disability in low income countries. *International Journal of Disability, Development and Education, 47,* 309–317.

Moll, L. C., Amanti, C., Neff, D., & Gonzalez, N. (1992). Funds of knowledge for teaching: Using a qualitative approach to connect homes and classrooms. *Theory into Practice, 31,* 132–141.

Moll, L. C., & Greenberg, J. (1990). Creating zones of possibilities: Combining social contexts for instruction. In L. C. Moll (Ed.), *Vygotsky and education* (pp. 319–348). Cambridge, UK: Cambridge University Press.

Monasch, R., & Boerma, J. T. (2004). Orphanhood and child care patterns in sub-Saharan Africa: An analysis of national surveys from 40 countries. *AIDS, 18*(Suppl 2), S55–S65.

Morley, D., & Woodland, M. (1988). *See how they grow: Monitoring child growth for appropriate health care in developing countries*. London, UK: MacMillan.

Mtonga, M. (2012). *Children's games and play in Zambia*. Lusaka, Zambia: University of Zambia Press.

Mukela, M. (2013). *The role of indigenous music and games in the promotion of cognitive development in Zambian children in Senanga and Shangombo Districts of Western Province* (Master's thesis). University of Zambia, Lusaka, Zambia. Retrieved from http://dspace.unza.zm:8080/xmlui/handle/123456789/3284

Mumba, P. (2000, July 24–28). *Democratisation of primary classrooms in Zambia: A case study of its implementation in a rural primary school in Mpika*. Paper presented at International Special Education Congress 2000, University of Manchester, UK. Retrieved from http://www.isec2000.org.uk/abstracts/papers_m/mumba_2.htm

Nabuzoka, D. (Ed.). (1986). *Reaching disabled children in Zambia: Reports and other documents on the Zambia National Campaign to Reach Disabled Children*. Lusaka, Zambia: Institute for African Studies, University of Zambia.

Nabuzoka, D. (1989). Individualised programme planning for home based education of mentally handicapped children in rural areas. In R. Serpell, D. Nabuzoka, & F. E. A.

Lesi (Eds.), *Early intervention, developmental disability, and mental handicap in Africa* (pp. 48–58). Lusaka, Zambia: Teresianum Press (for UNZA) & UNICEF.

Ng'andu, J., & Herbst, A. (2004). Lukwesa ne ciwa—The story of Lukwesa and Iciwa: Musical storytelling of the Bemba. *British Journal of Music, 21*, 41–61.

Nketia, J. H. K. (1963). *African music in Ghana: A survey of traditional forms.* Evanston, IL: Northwestern University Press, Northwestern University African Studies.

Nketia, J. H. K. (1973). The study of African and Afro-American music. *The Black Perspective in Music, 1*, 7–15.

Nsamenang, A. B. (2012). On researching the agency of Africa's young citizens: Issues, challenges, and prospects for identity development. In D. T. Slaughter-Defoe (Ed.), *Racial stereotyping and child development. Contributions to human development* (Vol. 25, pp. 90–104). Basel, Switzerland: Karger.

Nyota, S., & Mapara, J. (2008). Shona traditional children's games and play: Songs as indigenous ways of knowing. *The Journal of Pan African Studies, 2*, 189–202. Retrieved from http://www.amazon.com./shona-traditional-childrens-games-play/dp/B002132HU0

Oburu, P. O. (2009). HIV/AIDS generated caregiving burdens and the emergent two generation family structure in sub-Saharan Africa. *Bulletin of the International Society for Study of Behavioral Development (ISSBD), 56*, 7–9.

Oburu, P. O., & Palmerus, K. (2003). Parenting stress and self-reported discipline strategies of Kenyan caregiving grandmothers. *International Journal of Behavioral Development, 27*, 505–512.

Ogden, J., Esim, S., & Grown, C. (2006). Expanding the care continuum for HIV/AIDS: Bringing carers into focus. *Health Policy Plan, 21*(5), 333–342. doi:10.1093/heapol/czl025

Okonji, M. O. (1971). The effects of familiarity on classification. *Journal of Cross-Cultural Psychology, 2*, 39–49.

Okonji, M. O. (1980). Cognitive styles across cultures. In N. Warren (Ed.), *Studies in cross-cultural psychology* (Vol. 2, pp. 1–50). London, UK: Academic Press.

Okwany, A., Ngutuku, E., & Muhangi, A. (2011). *The role of knowledge and culture in child care in Africa: A sociological study of several ethnic groups in Kenya and Uganda.* Lewiston, NY: Edwin Mellen Press.

Oleke, C., Blystad, A., Rekdal, O. B., & Moland, K. M. (2007). Experiences of orphan care in Amach, Uganda: Assessing policy implications. *Journal of Social Aspects of AIDS, 4*, 532–543.

Pence, A., Evans, J. L., & Garcia, M. (2008). Introduction. In M. Garcia, A. Pence, & J. L. Evans (Eds.), *Africa's future, Africa's challenge: Early childhood care and development in sub-Saharan Africa* (pp. 1–7). Washington, DC: World Bank.

Prah, K. K., & Brock-Utne, B. (Eds.). (2009). *Multilingualism: An African advantage.* Cape Town, South Africa: Center for Advanced Studies of African Society (CASAS).

Rogoff, B. (2003). *The cultural nature of human development.* New York, NY: Oxford University Press.

Rose, P. (2003). Community participation in school policy and practice in Malawi: Balancing local knowledge, national policies and international agency priorities. *Compare, 33*, 47–64.

Serpell, R. (1986). Specialized centres and the local home community: Children with disabilities need them both. *International Journal of Special Education, 1*, 107–127.

Serpell, R. (1993). *The significance of schooling: Life-journeys in an African society.* Cambridge, UK: Cambridge University Press.

Serpell, R. (2008). Participatory appropriation and the cultivation of nurturance: A case study of African primary health science curriculum development. In P. R. Dasen & A. Akkari (Eds.), *Educational theories and practices from the "majority world"* (pp. 71–97). New Delhi, India: Sage.

Serpell, R. (2014). Promotion of literacy in Sub-Saharan Africa: Goals and prospects of CAPOLSA at the University of Zambia. *Human Technology, 10*(1), 23–39.

Serpell, R., & Jere-Folotiya, J. (2011). Basic education for children with special needs in Zambia: Progress and challenges in the translation of policy into practice. *Psychology and Developing Societies, 23,* 211–245.

Serpell, R., Mariga, L., & Harvey, K. (1993). Mental retardation in African countries: Conceptualization, services, and research. *International Review of Research in Mental Retardation, 19,* 1–39.

Serpell, R., Mumba, P., & Chansa-Kabali, T. (2011). Early educational foundations for the development of civic responsibility: An African experience. In C. A. Flanagan & B. D. Christens (Eds.), *New Directions for Child and Adolescent Development: No. 134. Youth civic development: Work at the cutting edge* (pp. 77–93). San Francisco, CA: Jossey-Bass.

Serpell, R., & Nsamenang, A. B. (2014). Locally relevant and quality ECCE programmes: Implications of research on indigenous African child development and socialization. *Early childhood care and education working papers series, 3.* Paris: UNESCO (ED.2013/WS/38). Retrieved from http://unesdoc.unesco.org/images/0022/002265/226564e.pdf

Sturmey, P., Thorburn, M. J., Brown, J. M., Reed, J., Kaur, J., & King, G. (1992). Portage guide to early intervention: Cross-cultural aspects and intra-cultural variability. *Child Care, Health and Development, 18,* 377–394.

Super, C. M., & Harkness, S. (2002). Culture structures the environment for development. *Human Development, 45,* 270–274.

United Nations Educational, Scientific, and Cultural Organization (UNESCO). (1990). *World declaration on education for all.* Retrieved from http://www.unesco.org/new/en/education/themes/leading-the-international-agenda/education-for-all/

United Nations (UN) General Assembly. (1989). *United Nations Convention on the Rights of the Child (UNCRC).* Retrieved from http://www.ohchr.org/en/professionalinterest/pages/crc.aspx

Walker, S. P., Wachs, T. D., Gardner, J. M., Lozoff, B., Wasserman, G. A., Pollitt, E., ... International Child Development Steering Group. (2007). Child development: Risk factors for adverse outcomes in developing countries. *Lancet, 369,* 145–157.

Weisner, T. S. (1997). Support for children and the African family crisis. In T. S. Weisner, C. Bradley, & P. L. Kilbride (Eds.), *African families and the crisis of social change* (pp. 20–44). Westport, CT: Bergin & Garvey.

WHO. (1983). *A manual on training disabled people in the community: Community-based rehabilitation for developing countries.* Geneva, Switzerland: Author.

Wober, M. (1975). *Psychology in Africa.* London, UK: International African Institute.

Yoshikawa, H., Weisner, T. S., Kalil, A., & Way, N. (2008). Mixing qualitative and quantitative research in developmental science. *Developmental Psychology, 44,* 344–354.

ROBERT SERPELL *is a professor of applied developmental psychology and coordinator of the Center for Promotion of Literacy in Sub-Saharan Africa (CAPOLSA) in the School of Humanities and Social Sciences, University of Zambia.*

KOFI MARFO *is a professor and founding director of the Institute for Human Development, Aga Khan University (South-Central Asia, East Africa, and the United Kingdom), and coleader of the Africa Child Development Research Capacity Building initiative.*

INDEX

Aase, A., 106
AAU. *See* Association of African Universities (AAU)
Abebe, T., 105, 106
Abubakar, A., 23–24, 25, 41, 80, 83, 84, 102
Acevedo, C., 63
Achebe, C., 67
Ada, A., 65
Adair, J. G., 15
Adjéi, K. K., 6, 10, 80
Adnams, C., 25
African child development field: African reflexivity, challenge of, 98; challenges for, 12–15, 98–101; contextual diversity, relevance, and practical importance, challenge of, 98–99; cross-sector integration of, 105–109; dimensions, intrinsically African, 103–105; indigenizing, challenge of, 14–15; intelligibility to African audiences, challenge of, 99–101; key features of, 98; linguistic hegemony, 12–13; marginalization of indigenous languages, 13–14
African developmental psychology: contextual relevance of, 8–10; intelligibility for local audiences, 10–12; motivating trends in, 4–12; Piaget's "genetic epistemology," 4–6; practical usefulness of, 8–10; search for universals, 4–8; testing cross-cultural validity of Western theories, 4–8
Africa's Future, Africa's Challenge: Early Childhood Care and Development in Sub-Saharan Africa, 107
Aikenhead, G. S., 52, 57
Akkari, A., 66
Akuj (God), 46
Akurut, H., 79, 82
Alant, E., 83
Alcock, K. J., 79, 81, 82, 87
Aldenkamp, A. P., 24
Allen, A. B., 33
Amae, 12

Amandi, C., 70
Amanti, C., 44, 49–50, 103
Amponsah, M., 44, 45, 47
Andrade, R., 71
Annis, R. C., 7
Antiretrovirals (ARVs), 25–30
Apule, B., 79, 82
Ardila, A., 79
ARVs. *See* Antiretrovirals (ARVs)
Asgharzadeh, A., 65
Assandé, N., 10, 80
Association of African Universities (AAU), 9
Astatke, H., 92
Atieno, M., 24
Atwoli, L., 31
Azuma, H., 12

Bachanas, P., 32
Badia, X., 84
Bagenda, D., 25, 31
Bahuchet, S., 7
Baillieu, N., 25
Banda, F., 14, 104
Bangirana, P., 25
Barnett, W. S., 74
Barry, O., 3
Barthélémy, D., 10, 80
Barton, D., 68
Behrman, J. R., 99, 107
Bellinger, D., 25
Bennish, M. L., 32
Bernstein, M., 80
Berry, J. W., 2, 6–8
Betancourt, H., 17
Bhana, A., 106
Bialystok, E., 13
Biersteker, L., 45, 47, 54, 56–57, 99–10
Black, M. M., 99, 107
Bland, R., 31–32
Bloch, C., 72
Blystad, A., 106
Boal, H. E., 25
Bodde, N., 24
Bodrova, E., 74

113

Boerma, J. T., 106
Boivin, M. J., 25, 30, 31, 33
Bond, V., 105
Boothby, L., 17
Bosl, W. J., 36
Boyd, J., 74
Boyes, M. E., 24, 33–36
Braadland, N., 106
Bradshaw, K., 25, 34
Brock-Utne, B., 104
Bronfenbrenner, U., 35
Broverman, S. A., 33
Brown, J. M., 106
Brown, R. I., 78
Bruner, J. S., 5, 8, 49
Buck, W. C., 25
Buck-Morss, S., 5
Busman, R. A., 33

Cabral de Mello, M., 99, 107
Calles, N. R., 31
Campain, N., 30, 31
Campbell, C., 106
Cancel, R., 14
Cannon, J., 62
Cao, H., 25
CAPOLSA. *See* Centre for Promotion of Literacy in Sub-Saharan Africa (CAPOLSA)
Carlson, J. S., 79
Carlsson, M. A., 45
Carter, J. A., 24
Case, R., 5–6
Cavalli-Sforza, L. L., 7
Caviness, A. C., 25
CDAZ. *See* Child Assessment Tool for Zambia (CDAZ)
Centre for Promotion of Literacy in Sub-Saharan Africa (CAPOLSA), 104
Chalamanda, F., 44, 45, 47
Chamvu, F., 87
Chansa-Kabali, T., 104, 105
Charlebois, E., 25
Charles, B., 106
Chart, H., 87
Chesang, K., 32
Cheung, Y. B., 107
Child assessment tests, in Zambia, 77–92: analysis of instrument design and validation, 84–91; approaches for adapting, 83–84; cross-cultural issues in, 79–83; instrument bias, 81; method bias, 80–81; overview, 78–79; Panga Munthu Test, 85–88; sample bias, 80–81; Tactile Pattern Reasoning, 89–91; ZamCAT, 88–91
Child Assessment Tool for Zambia (CDAZ), 82
Child Development Perspectives, 108
Chirwa, M. L., 33
Cluver, L. D., 24, 32–36
Cole, M., 2, 7–8, 15
Coleman, J. S., 9
Colette, C., 62
Communication: cooperative, 99–101; interdisciplinary and cross-sector, 101
Conway, B., 80
Cooper, P., 25
Cooperative communication, 99–101
Coovadia, A., 30
Coughenour, M., 51
Court, D., 9
Cox, C. M., 25
Craik, F. I. M., 13
Croome, N., 25, 34
Cross-cultural psychology, 2
Cueto, S., 107
Cultural psychology, 15
Cummins, J., 13
Curran, H. V., 67
Cutting, W. A. M., 30

Dabis, F., 25, 30
Daouda, K., 10, 80
Dasen, P. R., 2, 5–8, 10, 66, 80
Davidson, D. H., 12
Davies, A. G., 30
Dawson, J. L. M., 6
de Haan, M., 36
Dei, G., 65
Denton, F. K., 78
Deo-Gratias, H., 25, 30
Deregowski, J. B., 81–82
Devendra, A., 31
Devlin, A., 25
Dlamini, P. S., 33
Dolan, C. V., 79
Donaldson, M., 5
Dow, A., 25
Drabkin, A. S., 33
Drenth, P. J. D., 10

Drotar, D., 25, 31
Duracinsky, M., 33
Durkin, M. S., 79
Durojaiye, M. O. A., 10, 82
Dworin, J., 71
Dyer, C., 45, 51, 57
Dyk, R. B., 6

EAQEL study. *See* East Africa Quality in Early Learning (EAQEL) study
Early childhood care and education (ECCE), 62, 74
Early childhood development, care, and education (ECDCE), 107–108
Early childhood education (ECE), 43–57
Early literacy development study, 65–67
East Africa Quality in Early Learning (EAQEL) study, 64–65
ECCE. *See* Early childhood care and education (ECCE)
ECDCE. *See* Early childhood development, care, and education (ECDCE)
ECE. *See* Early childhood education (ECE)
ECE curriculum, for Turkana nomadic communities, 43–57: activities in rural centers, 47–49; cultural knowledge and practices, 49–57; ethnographic studies, 45–46; pedagogical value of indigenous knowledge, 52–57; Western models of, 44–49
Education for All (EFA), 62
Edwards, V., 14
EFA. *See* Education for All (EFA)
Egol, 48
Eley, B., 25
Eller, L. A., 25
Elliot, A. M., 79, 82
Eloff, I., 33
Engle, P. L., 99, 107
Enriquez, V. G., 12–13
Erny, P., 2
Esim, S., 106
Ettling, D., 82
Evans, J. L., 44, 45, 107
Ezeilo, B., 85

Family funds of knowledge, recognization of, 70–72
Faterson, H. F., 6

Fawzi, W. W., 25
Fennie, K. P., 33
Filteau, S., 31–32
Finestone, M., 33
Fink, G., 78, 88, 89, 91
Finn-Stevenson, M., 78
Floyd-Tenery, M., 70
Fobih, D. K., 6
Forsyth, B. W., 33
Fortes, M., 2
Fox-Rushby, J., 84
Frijda, N., 79
Fryers, T., 79
Funds of knowledge, 100

Gajdosik, C., 25
Garcia, M., 44, 45, 107
Gardner, F., 32, 33
Gardner, J. M., 107
Garrashi, H. H., 36
Geissler, P. W., 10
Gertler, P. J., 99, 107
Gilliam, W. S., 62
Giordani, B., 30, 33
Glazebrook, C., 30, 31
Glewwe, P., 107
Goldberg, L., 25
Gollan, T. H., 13
Gomby, D., 74
Gona, J., 36
Gonzales, R., 70
González, N., 44, 49–50, 70, 103
Goodenough, D. R., 6
Goodman, R., 30
Grant, I., 24
Grantham-McGregor, S., 107
Greeff, M., 33
Green, D. W., 13
Green, S. D. R., 30
Greenberg, J. B., 63, 71, 103
Greenfield, P. M., 5, 15, 79
Gridley, M. C., 104
Grigorenko, E. L., 10, 80, 87, 89
Grown, C., 106
Guay, L., 25
Gudyanga, S., 45, 47
Guo, Y., 32

Habtom, A., 44, 45, 47
Hambleton, R., 84
Hamilton, M., 68

Hardy, D. J., 24
Harkness, J. A., 84
Harkness, S., 3, 8, 44, 50, 103
Harris, D. B., 85
Hart, L., 87
Harvey, K., 106
Hassan, A., 23
Hatano, G., 81
Havlir, D. V., 25
Hawes, H., 105
Haynes, B., 10, 79
He, G., 33
Henderson, P. C., 106
Hennig, K., 52, 57
Herbst, A., 104
Herdman, M., 84
Herrero-Romero, R., 25, 34
Herrmann, S., 33
Heugh, K., 14
Hilliard, A. G., 80
HIV-infected parents, uninfected children of, 31–32
Holding, P. A., 24, 25, 36, 80, 81, 83, 84, 87
Holzemer, W. L., 33
Home and school literacy practices interface in rural Zimbabwe study, 63–64
Horowitz, F. D., 14
Huang, L., 33
Hudson, W., 82
Hughes, P., 44
Hui, L., 15
Hwang, K. K., 2
Hyland, N. B., 33

ICDSG. *See* International Child Development Steering Group (ICDSG)
Indigenous languages, marginalization of, 13–14
Indigenous orientation, 14
Indigenous psychology, 2, 14
Interdisciplinary and cross-sector communication, 101
International Child Development Steering Group (ICDSG), 107
Irvine, S. H., 10
Isquith, P. K., 36

Jahoda, G., 2, 79
Jaramillo, A., 44
Jarvin, L., 87

Jegede, O. J., 52, 57
Jere, J., 87
Jere-Folotiya, J., 10, 79, 87, 104, 106
Johnson, T. P., 84
Jones, S., 62
Jukes, M. C. H., 89

Kabiru, M., 45
Kabue, M. M., 25
Kagitcibasi, C., 8, 14
Kalil, A., 108
Kalyesubula, I., 25, 31
Kamau, J. W., 30, 31
Kameka, G., 44, 45, 47
Kammerer, B., 36
Kan, E., 10, 80
Kangethe, R., 31
Kapiriri, L., 99, 107
Karoly, L. A., 62
Karp, S., 6
Kathuria, R., 86, 88
Kaufman, A. S., 89
Kaufman, N. L., 89
Kaufman Pattern Reasoning, 89, 91
Kaur, J., 106
Kawagley, A. O., 52
Kazembe, P. N., 31
Kazungu, S. D., 36
KDC. *See* Kilifi Developmental Checklist (KDC)
Kemp, S. L., 89
Kenga, S., 84
Kenny, D. A., 10
Kenyatta, J., 67
Kessler, S., 104
Ketron, J., 80
Kidder, D., 32
Kihara, M., 24, 36
Kilbride, J. C., 106
Kilbride, P. L., 106
Kilburn, M. R., 62
Kilifi Developmental Checklist (KDC), 84
Kim, U., 2
Kiminyo, D. M., 6
King, G., 106
Kinyanda, E., 30
Kirk, U., 89
Kirova, A., 52, 57
Kitsao-Wekulo, P., 23, 80, 83, 84
Kiziri-Mayengo, R., 25

Kjorholt, A. T., 105
Kohi, T. W., 33
Korkman, M., 89
Kouame, K., 10
Kouamé, K., 80
Krätli, S., 45, 57
Krebs, G., 32
Kuper, H., 31
Kuria, W., 31

Lagmay, A. V., 12
Lalanne, C., 33
Lapidus, L. B., 82
Lawn, J. E., 24
Lebra, T. S., 12
Le Doaré, K., 31–32
Leong, D. J., 74
Lepage, P., 25, 30
LeVine, R. A., 3, 108
LeVine, S., 3, 108
Lewa, N., 84
Li, X., 32, 33
Linguistic hegemony, 12–13
Lipsitz, G., 104
Literacy practices in local environments, promotion of, 73
Literacy-rich environment creation, by parents, 72–73
Lopez, S. R., 17
Lozoff, B., 24, 107
Lule, S., 79, 82
Lundy, S., 36
Lyytinen, H., 104

MacGinitie, W. H., 82
MacNaughton, G., 44
Maenner, M., 79
Magolda, B. M. B., 65
Maimane, S., 106
Makawa, A., 31
Makin, J., 33
Makoae, L. N., 33
Mallal, S., 33
Malmberg, L.-E., 78
Mandyata, J. M., 82
Manji, K., 25
Mapara, J., 104
Marfo, K., 1, 3–4, 9, 14–15, 17, 22, 45, 54, 56–57, 97–100, 106–108, 112
Marianna, B., 45–46, 49–50
Mariga, L., 106

Marum, L., 25
Maslow, A., 68
Matafwali, B., 36, 77, 78, 82, 86, 88, 89, 91, 96, 101
Mathai, M., 31
Mazrui, A., 15
Mbatia, R., 32
Mbiti, J. S., 15
McCabe, J. M., 51
McCollum, E. D., 25
McConkey, R., 106
McGrath, N., 25
McKinnon, E., 33
McNaughton, S., 65
McPhee, C., 78
MDGs. *See* Millennium Development Goals (MDGs)
Meeks Gardner, J., 24
Melhuish, E., 78
Menon, A., 30, 31
Meyer, M. S., 80
Mid Upper Arm Circumference (MUAC), 89
Millennium Development Goals (MDGs), 44, 62
Mingat, A., 44
Mitchell, D. M., 78
Mithwani, S., 84
Mkala, T., 36
Mlama, P., 11
Mokili, J. K. L., 30
Moland, K. M., 106
Moll, L. C., 44, 49–50, 63, 70, 71, 103
Monasch, R., 106
Moore, D. J., 24
Morley, D., 105
Moucheraud, C., 78, 88, 91
Moumouni, A., 15
Mphole, P., 106
Mpofu, E., 10, 78
Msamanga, G. I., 25
Msango, H., 82
Msellati, P., 25, 30
Mshelua, A. Y., 82
Mtonga, M., 11, 104
MUAC. *See* Mid Upper Arm Circumference (MUAC)
Mudaala-Simfukwe, E., 82
Muhangi, A., 99
Muhangi, L., 79, 82
Mukela, M., 104

Mumba, P., 105
Munachaka, J. C., 104
Mundy-Castle, A. C., 82
Mung'ala-Odera, V., 81, 87
Mupuala, A., 25
Musisi, S., 30
Mwamunye, B., 36
Mwaniki, M. K., 24
Mwansa, A. B., 82
Mwaura, P. A. M., 3, 78
Mweru, M., 63

Nabuzoka, D., 106
Nair, Y., 106
Nampijja, M., 79, 82
Nankunda, H., 44, 45, 47
Nassali, A., 25, 31
Neff, D., 49–50, 103
Nell, V., 79
NEPSY Block Construction, 89, 91
Neville, B. G., 36
Newell, M.-L., 31–32
Newton, C. R., 24, 25, 36
Newton, C. R. J. C., 81, 87
Ng'andu, J., 104
Ngaruiya, S., 45, 47
Ng'asike, J., 43, 45, 47, 50, 54, 60, 99, 102–103
Ngenda, I., 88
Ngoma, M. S., 30, 31
Ngugi, J., 13
Ngugi wa Thiongo, 13
Ngutuku, E., 99
Ngwaru, J. M., 14, 61, 63, 65, 67–68, 71–72, 76, 99–100, 102–103
Nicholson, J., 106
Nickse, R., 65
Njenga, A., 45
Njoroge, L., 63, 65, 71
Nketia, J. H. K., 104
Nokes, C., 10
Nolan, D., 33
Nsamenang, A. B., 15, 45, 54, 56, 65–66, 105, 107
Nsolo, 90–91
Ntarangwi, M., 57
Nyanungo, K. R. L., 78
Nyota, S., 104

Obiero, E., 84
Oburu, P. O., 106
Ogbonna-Ohuche, R. O., 6
Ogden, J., 106
Ogwang-Odhiambo, R. A., 33
Oka, E., 33
Okatcha, F., 10
Okonji, M. O., 6–7, 81, 103
Okwany, A., 99
Oleke, C., 106
Olness, K., 25, 31
Oluga, M., 63
Olver, R. R., 5
Omari, I. M., 82
Operario, D., 32
Opolot, J. A., 82
Orkin, M., 24, 33, 35, 36
Otaala, B., 6
Owoe, P. J., 6

Page, C., 33
Palmerus, K., 106
Pals, S., 32
Panga Munthu Test (PMT), 85–88: core features of, 85; development and validation of, 85–88; Zambia academic achievement test and, 87
Parent, J., 32
Parent–teacher empowerment, 65–67
Parents, involvement in early schooling in Africa, 61–74: EAQEL study, 64–65; early literacy development study, 65–67; empowerment of, 67–70; family funds of knowledge, 70–72; literary practices study, 63–64; and literacy-rich environments, 72–73; overview, 62–63; parent–teacher empowerment study, 65–67; policy recommendations, 73–74
Parra-Castaneda, K., 25, 34
Pascual-Leone, J., 5
Paul, J. L., 15
Pauls, D. L., 80
Pediatric HIV population, in Sub-Saharan Africa, 105–107: biomedical risk factors, 24–31; conceptual models for, 34–36; educational outcomes, 31; future directions for, 34–36; HIV-related stigma, 33–34; instruments for studying, 36; longitudinal approaches to studying, 36–37; maternal psychosocial functioning, 33; mental health, 30–31; neurocognitive outcomes, 25, 30; orphanhood, 33;

overview, 24; poverty and, 32; studies on, 26–29; use of antiretrovirals, 30
Pence, A. R., 3, 44, 45, 47, 65, 107–108
Petersen, I., 106
Phiri, J. T., 82
Piaget's "genetic epistemology," 4–6
Picture Vocabulary Test (PPVT), 89
PMT. *See* Panga Munthu Test (PMT)
Pollitt, E., 24, 107
Poortinga, Y. H., 2, 8, 23, 80
Potterton, J., 25, 30
PPVT. *See* Picture Vocabulary Test (PPVT)
Prah, K. K., 104
Price-Williams, D. R., 2, 4
Prince, R., 10
Psychology in Africa, 2
Psychology of Literacy, The, 7
Puffer, E. S., 33

Ratner, C., 15
Rave, W., 104
Reading for Children (RfC), 64–65
Reading to Learn (RtL), 64–65
Reed, J., 106
Rekdal, O. B., 106
Rendon, P., 70
Retschitzki, J., 90
Reynolds, A., 62
RfC. *See* Reading for Children (RfC)
Richter, L., 32, 107
Rivera, A., 70
Robins, J., 25
Rochat, T., 32
Rogoff, B., 44, 49–50, 54, 81, 103
Rose, D., 63
Rose, P., 107
Roselli, M., 79
RtL. *See* Reading to Learn (RtL)
Ruel, T. D., 25

Saavedra, E., 71
Saling-pusa, 12
Sameroff, A. E., 35
Sammons, P., 78
Sampa, F., 104
Samuelsson, I. P., 45
Schooling: linguistic hegemony's effects on, 12–13; and marginalization of indigenous languages, 13–14
Schuurman, M. M., 79
Scribner, S., 7

SDQ. *See* Strengths and Difficulties Questionnaire (SDQ)
Sebatane, E., 45, 47
Segall, M. H., 2, 8
Senechal, C., 7
Serpell, R., 1–3, 6–12, 17, 22, 36, 56, 77, 79–83, 85–88, 92, 96–97, 100–101, 104–107, 112
Seth, P., 32
Sherman, B., 25, 31
Sherr, L., 24, 25, 32, 34, 35
Shweder, R. A., 2, 15
Siegler, R. S., 5
Sikkema, K. J., 33
Sinha, D., 2, 14
Sipsma, H., 33
Siraj-Blatchford, I., 78
Smith, K., 44
Smith, L., 25
Social selfhood, 15
Speicher, N. A., 65
Stashko, A. L., 33
Stein, A., 32
Stemler, S. E., 87
Sternberg, R. J., 10, 80
Stevenson, J., 36
Stewart, A., 25
Strengths and Difficulties Questionnaire (SDQ), 30–31
Strupp, B., 107
Sturmey, P., 106
Sullivan, E. V., 24
Super, C. M., 3, 8, 44, 50, 103
Svilar, G., 25
Swadener, B. B., 104
Swadener, E., 45
Sylva, K., 78

Tactile Pattern Reasoning, 89–91
Taggart, B., 78
Taljaardt, E., 83
Tanzer, N. K., 80
Taylor, H. G., 36
Tchombe, T. M. S., 54, 56, 65–66
Tesner, H., 83
Thorburn, M. J., 106
Tobin, J. J., 12
Tomkins, A., 32
Traditional food processing, in Tanzania, 70
Triplett, K., 33
Tronick, E., 25

Turkana calendar, in ECE curriculum, 51–54
Turkana cultural knowledge and practices, 49–57: vs. formal school science content, 55–56; with livestock, 50–51; Turkana calendar, 51–54

UNCRC. *See* United Nations Convention on the Rights of Children (UNCRC)
UNESCO. *See* United Nations Educational, Scientific, and Cultural Organization (UNESCO)
United Nations Convention on the Rights of Children (UNCRC), 44
United Nations Educational, Scientific, and Cultural Organization (UNESCO), 44, 62, 74, 107
Uys, L. R., 33

Van Baar, A., 24, 25
Vance, D. E., 24
van de Koppel, J. M. H., 7
Van de Perre, P., 25, 30
van der Maas, H. L. N., 79
Van de Vijver, F. J. R., 23–25, 80, 84
Van Goethem, C., 25, 30
Van Rie, A., 25
Velez-Ibanez, C., 71
Vernon, P. E., 10, 82
Vygotsky, L. S., 7, 44, 49–50, 65

Wachira, P., 45
Wachs, T. D., 24, 107
Walberg, H., 62
Walker, S. P., 24, 106, 107
Wang, H., 33
Wang, M., 62
Wanless, S. R., 25
Wasserman, G. A., 24, 107
Way, N., 108
Weber, E., 24

Weisner, T. S., 44, 50, 105, 106, 108
Were, E. O., 36
Westerholm, J., 104
Whitehead, N., 30
Whitmore, K., 71
Wicherts, J. M., 79
Williams, A. B., 33
Witkin, H. A., 6, 7
Wiznitzer, M., 25
Wober, M., 2–3, 6, 8, 83, 103
Wong, J. K., 25
Wood, F. B., 80
Woodland, M., 105
Woods, S. P., 24
World Declaration on Education for All, 62
Wu, D. Y. H., 12

Yalukanda, C., 104
Yang, K. S., 2
Yesufu, T. M., 9
Yoshikawa, H., 108
Young, M. E., 99, 107

Zambia academic achievement test (ZAT), 87
Zambia Child Assessment Tool (ZamCAT), 88–91: development and validation of, 89–91; domain areas of, 88–89; subtests of, 89–91; Tactile Pattern Reasoning, 89–91
Zambia Early Childhood Project (ZECP), 88
ZamCAT. *See* Zambia Child Assessment Tool (ZamCAT)
ZAT. *See* Zambia academic achievement test (ZAT)
ZECP. *See* Zambia Early Childhood Project (ZECP)
Zeitlin, M., 3
Zhang, Y., 36
Zigler, E. F., 62, 78
Zuilkowski, S. S., 78, 88, 89, 91

OTHER TITLES AVAILABLE IN THE
NEW DIRECTIONS FOR CHILD AND ADOLESCENT DEVELOPMENT SERIES
Lene Arnett Jensen and Reed W. Larson, Editors-in-Chief
William Damon, Founding Editor-in-Chief

For a complete list of back issues, please visit www.josseybass.com/go/ndcad

CAD145 *Rereading Personal Narrative and Life Course*
Brian Schiff, Editor
Rereading Personal Narrative and Life Course is a reflection on the place of narrative interpretation in life course developmental theory. As a point of departure, we begin from Bertram Joseph Cohler's (1938–2012) contribution to our understanding of developmental psychology. Cohler's (1982) visionary chapter Personal Narrative and Life Course was one of the first published manuscripts in psychology on the process of storytelling for establishing selfhood and identity and one of the first essays on what would later become narrative psychology. Thirty years after its publication, there is now a large literature on the role of narrative in human development. But, the themes that Cohler advanced are still fresh and future oriented, prescient of an emerging interpretive developmental psychology. This volume features exciting chapters by the leading figures in narrative psychology reflecting on the narrative character of the life course in early childhood (Peggy J. Miller, Eva Chian-Hui Chen, & Megan Olivarez), adolescence (Tilmann Habermas & Neşe Hatiboğlu), emerging adulthood (Phillip L. Hammack & Erin Toolis), midlife (Dan P. McAdams), and old age (Amia Lieblich). Mark Freeman provides further context and insight in the epilogue. Read together, the chapters form a comprehensive description of narrative's origins in childhood conversations and the multiple uses that narrative is put to as lives unfold over developmental and historical time. The volume is a touchstone text in human development and an entryway for psychologists who would like to rethink their approach to development through the lens of a narrative perspective that is sensitive to interpretation and context in human lives.
ISBN 978-11189-84888

CAD144 *Positive and Negative Outcomes of Sexual Behaviors*
Eva S. Lefkowitz, Sara A. Vasilenko, Editors
Developing healthy sexual behaviors is critical to adolescents' wellbeing. Yet both research and sexuality education programs have typically emphasized negative outcomes, including sexually transmitted infections and pregnancy. However, sexual behavior may have broader positive implications for physical health, mental health, intimate relationships, and identity development. To fully understand the impact of sexual behavior on adolescents, we need to understand not only risk behavior processes, but also potential positive outcomes. In addition, the impact of sexual behavior is not universal, but may differ based on individuals' demographic, relational, contextual, and attitudinal factors. The chapters in this volume provide a framework for understanding the complex role of sexual behavior in adolescents' lives, with a specific focus on the roles of sexual minority status, internet-based sexual experiences, relationship context, and sexual

learning through formal and informal sex education in determining the outcomes of sexual behavior. As a whole, this volume provides a nuanced, multidimensional understanding of the role of sexual behavior in shaping adolescents' development and well-being, important directions for future research, and recommendations for sexuality education, prevention, and intervention programs.
ISBN 978-11189-30373

CAD143 **Pathways to Adulthood for Disconnected Young Men in Low-Income Communities**
Kevin Roy, Nikki Jones, Editors
Increased economic inequality threatens already precarious pathways to adulthood for young disadvantaged men. While young men from more stable, middle-class backgrounds can experiment with more autonomy and self-exploration as they transition to adulthood, young disadvantaged men often lose ground over this developmental period. Young men of color who come of age in urban neighborhoods must often contend with ongoing violence and the encroachment of the criminal justice system in their daily lives. These challenging circumstances alter parenting strategies and transitions to adulthood for this group. Parents who want to protect their sons from the threat of violence or incarceration may exile them from their home neighborhoods altogether, while young men who remain in these neighborhoods must learn to manage the ever-increasing surveillance of law enforcement and the mounting pressures that come along with adultification. As the chapters in this volume demonstrate, young, disadvantaged men from urban neighborhoods face a unique set of challenges and constraints as they transition to adulthood. Yet, these challenges are not always contained by place. Research among Latino and white disadvantaged men in non-urban settings highlights the pressures that come along with fatherhood for disadvantaged men. In contrast to popular understandings of absent or disengaged fathers, findings reveal how fatherhood and increasing levels of *inter*dependence during early adulthood can buffer men as they make the difficult transition to adulthood. The innovative field-based research featured in this volume illuminates the contexts, processes, and meanings in life pathways for disadvantaged men as they move from adolescence into adulthood and should help to inform policies and practices directed at minimizing their marginalization from mainstream society.
ISBN 978-11188-94071

NEW DIRECTIONS FOR CHILD AND ADOLESCENT DEVELOPMENT
ORDER FORM SUBSCRIPTION AND SINGLE ISSUES

DISCOUNTED BACK ISSUES:

Use this form to receive 20% off all back issues of *New Directions for Child and Adolescent Development*. All single issues priced at **$23.20** (normally $29.00).

TITLE	ISSUE NO.	ISBN
_____	_____	_____
_____	_____	_____
_____	_____	_____

Call 1-800-835-6770 or see mailing instructions below. When calling, mention the promotional code JBNND to receive your discount. For a complete list of issues, please visit www.josseybass.com/go/ndcad

SUBSCRIPTIONS: (1 YEAR, 4 ISSUES)

☐ New Order   ☐ Renewal

U.S.	☐ Individual: $89	☐ Institutional: $416
CANADA/MEXICO	☐ Individual: $89	☐ Institutional: $456
ALL OTHERS	☐ Individual: $113	☐ Institutional: $490

Call 1-800-835-6770 or see mailing and pricing instructions below.
Online subscriptions are available at www.onlinelibrary.wiley.com

ORDER TOTALS:

Issue / Subscription Amount: $ _____
Shipping Amount: $ _____
(for single issues only – subscription prices include shipping)
Total Amount: $ _____

SHIPPING CHARGES:
First Item $6.00
Each Add'l Item $2.00

(No sales tax for U.S. subscriptions. Canadian residents, add GST for subscription orders. Individual rate subscriptions must be paid by personal check or credit card. Individual rate subscriptions may not be resold as library copies.)

BILLING & SHIPPING INFORMATION:

☐ **PAYMENT ENCLOSED:** *(U.S. check or money order only. All payments must be in U.S. dollars.)*

☐ **CREDIT CARD:**   ☐ VISA   ☐ MC   ☐ AMEX

Card number _____ Exp. Date _____
Card Holder Name _____ Card Issue # _____
Signature _____ Day Phone _____

☐ **BILL ME:** *(U.S. institutional orders only. Purchase order required.)*

Purchase order # _____
Federal Tax ID 13559302 • GST 89102-8052

Name _____
Address _____
Phone _____ E-mail _____

Copy or detach page and send to: **John Wiley & Sons, One Montgomery Street, Suite 1000, San Francisco, CA 94104-4594**

Order Form can also be faxed to: **888-481-2665**

PROMO JBNND

Stay Informed with Wiley Publications

The Brown University Child and Adolescent Behavior Letter

12 issues for $199 **SAVE 50%!**
$99.50 (print) $89.50 (electronic)

Stay current with the news, research, clinical studies, and information you need to know in order to diagnose and treat psychiatric, behavioral, and developmental problems. Every issue is filled with practical applications, new therapies, prevention techniques, and research findings on issues seen in children and adolescent patients.
www.childadolescentbehavior.com

The Brown University Child and Adolescent Psychopharmacology Update

12 issues for $199 **SAVE 50%!**
$99.50 (print) $89.50 (electronic)

The latest news and information on children and adolescents' psychotropic medication—new drugs, new uses, typical doses, side effects, interactions, generic vs. name brand, reports on new research, and new indications for existing medications. Also includes case studies, industry news, abstracts of current research, and patient medication handouts.
www.childadolescentpsychopharm.com

The Brown University Psychopharmacology Update

12 issues for $199 **SAVE 50%!**
$99.50 (print) $89.50 (electronic)

These psychotropic drug updates help you stay current with the latest therapeutic treatments. You'll get bias-free information on new drugs in the pipeline, the latest evidence for a particular drug treatment, a newly discovered side effect, reports on drug interactions, and the latest FDA information.
www.psychopharmacologyupdate.com

New Directions for Youth Development

4 issues for $89 **SAVE 15%!** $75.65 (print or electronic)

This acclaimed periodical presents the latest theory, practice and research on youth development. Past topics include youth mentoring, threat and terror, immigrant youth, afterschool time, community building, and youth leadership.

Alcoholism & Drug Abuse Weekly

48 issues for $695 **SAVE 50%!**
$347.50 (print) $277.50 (electronic)

This weekly delivers all the latest news, trends, opportunities, and efficiencies to improve your quality of treatment—and your bottom line.

ADAW is filled with the latest information on national trends and developments in funding and policy issues, legislation, treatment, prevention, avoiding relapse, and research—anything that affects managing your program and caring for your clients.
www.alcoholismdrugabuseweekly.com

New Directions for Child and Adolescent Development

4 issues for $89 **SAVE 15%!** $75.65 (print or electronic)

The latest scholarship from the field of child and adolescent development. Topics include social, cognitive, educational, emotional, biological, and socio-cultural issues that bear on children and youth, as well as issues in research methodology and other domains.

Mental Health Weekly

48 issues for $699 **SAVE 50%!**
$347.50 (print) $277.50 (electronic)

This premier weekly publication brings you the latest information on fundamental issues, such as practice trends, state funding and policy issues, litigation, federal legislation and policy, workforce news, program success stories, and innovative practices—everything you need to stay informed and manage your practice.
www.mentalhealthweeklynews.com

SUBSCRIBE TODAY
Call 888.378.2537. Use promo code PSY14 and get discounted subscription rates—see below.